ACTIVATOR

NEXT

Tadashi Shiozawa
Adam Martinelli

KINSEIDO

Kinseido Publishing Co., Ltd.

3-21 Kanda Jimbo-cho, Chiyoda-ku,

Tokyo 101-0051, Japan

First published 2023 by Kinseido Publishing Co., Ltd.

Design   Nampoosha Co., Ltd.
Illustrasions   Toru Igarashi

Images Credits

Unit 1 © Blackzheep | Dreamstime.com, © Nopparat Khokthong | Dreamstime.com

Unit 2 © Carrienelson1 | Dreamstime.com

Unit 4 © Rodrigo Reyes | Dreamstime.com, © Wisconsinart | Dreamstime.com

Unit 5 © Leo Daphne | Dreamstime.com, © Lequint | Dreamstime.com

Unit 8 © Bigtunaonline | Dreamstime.com

Unit 9 © Sean Pavone | Dreamstime.com, © Phanthit Malisuwan | Dreamstime.com

Unit 10 © Joe Sohm | Dreamstime.com

Unit 11 © Dana Rothstein | Dreamstime.com

Unit 12 © Tktktk | Dreamstime.com, © Ekaterinabelova | Dreamstime.com

Unit 13 © Tktktk | Dreamstime.com, © Bestravelvideo .com | Dreamstime.com

Unit 14 © Pressureua | Dreamstime.com, © Jwijayaratne | Dreamstime.com

Unit 15 © James Group Studios, Inc. | Dreamstime.com

🎧 音声ファイル無料ダウンロード

https://www.kinsei-do.co.jp/download/4178

この教科書で 🎧 DL 00 の表示がある箇所の音声は、上記 URL または QR コードにて無料でダウンロードできます。自習用音声としてご活用ください。

▶ PC からのダウンロードをお勧めします。スマートフォンなどでダウンロードされる場合は、ダウンロード前に「解凍アプリ」をインストールしてください。

▶ URL は、検索ボックスではなくアドレスバー (URL 表示覧) に入力してください。

▶ お使いのネットワーク環境によっては、ダウンロードできない場合があります。

◎ CD 00　左記の表示がある箇所の音声は、教室用 CD（Class Audio CD）に収録されています。

はしがき

Activator Next は *Activator* シリーズの最新版です。日本の次世代の学習者が関心のある最新のトピックを扱い、日本人英語学習者の7割を占めると言われる false beginners（疑似初心者、つまり長く勉強しているが、いつまでも初心者のレベルから抜け出せない学習者）のために書かれた大学生用総合英語教材です。

Activator Next は、先行シリーズの *Activator*、*New Activator*、*Global Activator* 以上に消極的な英語学習者に「挑戦」します。彼らが本来持っているコミュニケーションへの内発的動機を「活性化」させ、その楽しさと、可能性を実感してもらうことが本書の目的です。本書は学習者たちが常に「自分たちに関係すること」を英語で話し、聞き、読み、書かざるをえないようなユニット構成になっています。しかも、それぞれの言語活動は、シンプルで「有意味性」と多様性に富んでいますので、消極的な大学生でも自然と自ら言語活動に取り組むはずです。

Activator Next の特徴は自然に小さな笑いを誘うダイアログやリスニング、好奇心をくすぐる読み物やコミュニケーションストラテジー訓練などです。特に、本書が前三作と異なるのは、**Quick Search On the Web** というネットを使った発展的な情報収集活動を取り入れたことです。現在の大学生世代の得意とするコンピュータやスマートフォンを使って、主体的な協働学習を授業内に取り組むことも可能です。

Activator Next は教員にとっても user-friendly です。各アクティビティの指示文はシンプルで具体的であり、例文が添えてあります。各エクササイズの指示文を英語で読み上げるだけで、学習者らは自然と言語活動に入り込み、あちこちで笑いが起こるような仕組みになっています。教授用資料では、部分ディクテーション用の教材や各章ごとに簡単な Quiz を提供します。データでのご用意もありますので編集してご利用いただけます。

最後に、本書を使う上での重要な留意点を記します。本書は、言語活動中心の授業展開となりますので、可能であれば、学習者にはペアで座るよう指示してください。また、学習者のニーズとレベルに応じて各活動は取捨選択してください。全てを行う必要はありません。リスニングやリーディングは global listening、skimming、scanning などを大いに奨励してください。学習者は細かい点まで理解する必要は全くありません。リズミカルに授業を展開すれば1ユニットを90分で完結することが可能です。学習者のレベルによっては通年教材として、2回の授業で1章ずつ進むのも良いでしょう。

本書を利用して、false beginners であっても「自分の英語」（My English）を使う楽しさと可能性を実感してもらい、結果的に英語コミュニケーション遂行力も大いに伸ばしていただきたいと思います。

著者

Introduction

Activator Next is a multi-skilled, function-situation based textbook wholly written for Japanese college-aged learners of English, who may be identified as "false beginners." They have studied English for a long time, but their communication capability and confidence level remain at an elementary level. All they need seems to be opportunities to use the language and feel the joy of global communication.

Activator Next, like its predecessors *Activator*, *New Activator*, and *Global Activator*, also keeps the tradition of challenging "passive learners" and not allowing them to sit quietly and do nothing in class. Task-based, fun, and motivating exercises throughout the course with highly relevant topics to the life of Japanese college students will "activate" their desires to communicate in English. Students will experience the pleasure of communication and build confidence in using English in a meaningful way. Non-threatening and highly personalized activities will enable passive learners to use target expressions in a meaningful and communicative way. The learners will assuredly leave the classroom with a sense of achievement and satisfaction.

Activator Next features dialogues and listening materials that naturally elicit small laughs, as well as short, interesting reading materials and communication strategy training exercises. In particular, this book differs from the previous three books by incorporating **Quick Search on the Web**, an activity using the Internet for gathering further information, which also allows students to engage in independent, collaborative learning in the classroom using computers and smart phones, a specialty of Gen Z and younger generations.

Activator Next is teacher-friendly too. With simple and clear directions accompanied with examples, learners are naturally engaged in the language activities, with a few chuckles here and there. Teaching materials include additional partial dictation materials and a short quiz for each chapter (in digital format). These materials can be freely edited and used.

Suggestions

It is important that the learners sit in pairs most of the time to make the best use of *Activator Next*. Most activities are designed to be conducted in pairs or groups so that the students have ample opportunity to practice interacting in English. With *Activator Next*, the students do most of the talking, not the teacher. Each unit can be completed within a 90-minute lesson; however, depending on the level or creativity of the learners, it could be conducted in two separate lessons. *Activa-*

tor Next is designed to be taught by either native or non-native speakers of English. Please make the best use of yourself as a native or non-native teacher. And most importantly, please have fun teaching using *Activator Next* with younger generations. It is designed that way. Some features of each language activity are as follows.

Brainstorm
Each unit starts with a brainstorming introduction exercise with highly personalized questions.

Dialogue
Learners practice the first part of the dialogue and replace parts of it to fit their own situation so that the dialogue becomes more meaningful. As a short listening exercise, the rest of the conversation with some surprising conclusions follows.

Expressions
Five basic target expressions are provided.

Interactive Practice
Three sets of some controlled, interactive, and communicative exercises follow the target expressions. The type of exercise varies from unit to unit.

Quick Search on the Web
If time and situation allow, learners are encouraged to use the Internet to find more information on the topic and share it with their classmates.

Communication Strategy
A variety of communication strategy training exercises are provided.

Active Listening
Learners listen to highly interesting, often entertaining listening materials followed by a variety of comprehension questions. Additional cloze test materials can be used here.

Active Reading
A short interesting and thought-provoking passage on the theme of each unit is provided. Learners are NOT expected to understand all of the words or expressions. Various comprehension exercises follow each reading.

Quick Search on the Web
Another information search activity relevant to the topic of the reading material is provided.

Activator
Highly communicative and interactive (and often open-ended) exercises conclude each unit. Some optional challenging discussion exercises are also provided.

Activator Next

Contents

College Life

Focus

Getting to Know Each Other

 ## Brainstorm

A Pair up and talk about yourself and your partner. Examples are shown in [   ].

1. *A:* May I ask your name?

   B: Sure, it's _____. And your name is?   [Shota / Miki]

2. *A:* Where did you go to high school?

   B: I went to _____ High. How about you?   [Tokiwadai / Karasuno]

3. *A:* How did you like your high school life?

   B: Oh, _____   [I loved it / it was OK]

   because _____.

   [I had many good friends / I didn't like the school rules]

4. *A:* How do you like to spend your free time?

   B: I like to _____.   [sleep / go mountain climbing]

B Switch Roles. This time add one or two extra comments. See the example below. Go over 1-4 above again. Below is an example for exercise number four.

   A: How do you like to spend your free time?
   B: I like to play video games.
   A: Hey, me too. What is your favorite game?
   B: I love Final Fantasy 16.
   A: Oh, I love that game. Maybe we should play together.
   B: ....

 # Dialogue 🎧 DL 02   💿 CD1-02

Yuta met Christen, an international student from the U.S., in the college Aikido club meeting for new students. Role-play the dialogue with your partner. Then switch roles and practice again.

Yuta: You must be <u>Christen</u> from <u>Ohio</u>.

Christen: You know my name?

Yuta: Yes. <u>Adam-senpai</u> told me that you're coming.

Christen: Good. I'd like to watch you guys practice today.

Yuta: No problem. You can practice with us if you like.

Christen: Really? That would be great. Can I ask your name?

Yuta: Oh, sorry. My name is <u>Yutaro</u>. Just call me <u>Yuta</u>.

Christen: OK. Nice to meet you, <u>Yuta</u>.

A Ask at least two questions about the dialogue to your partner. Take turns.

B Replace the underlined parts with your own information and practice the conversation again. Be original and creative. Try to add a few more lines at the end.

C Listen to the rest of the conversation and answer the questions.

🎧 DL 03   💿 CD1-03

1. What is Christen majoring in?

2. Is Christen interested in Japanese manga and anime?

3. What does Christen want to know about Japan?

4. Where do many freshmen and sophomores in American colleges live?

5. What does Yuta do on Sundays?

 **Expressions**

A Practice each dialogue with your partner.

1. *A:* **What are you majoring in?**
   B: I'm majoring in <u>economics.</u>

2. *A:* **Do you live in your own apartment or with your family?**
   B: I live <u>alone in my apartment</u>.

3. *A:* **What do you do in your free time?**
   B: I either <u>listen to music</u> or <u>play video games</u>.

4. *A:* **How do you like this university so far?**
   B: <u>I love it</u>. <u>The campus is pretty, and people are friendly</u>.

5. *A:* **Are you in any school clubs or societies?**
   B: No, but I'm thinking about joining <u>the karate club</u>.

B Replace the underlined words with your own words and practice again.

 Interactive Practice

A Expand your expressions. Role-play the dialogue with your partner using the appropriate words listed below. Do NOT write until you finish roleplaying.

where	*ask*	*in*	*love*	*good*

1. *A:* How're you doing?　　*B:* Pretty (　　　　). Thank you.

2. *A:* May I (　　　　) your name?　　*B:* Sure. My name is Yuto.

3. *A:* What is your major?　　*B:* I'm majoring (　　　　) psychology.

4. *A:* (　　　　) did you go to high school?　　*B:* I went to Karasuno High School in Miyagi.

5. *A:* What do you do in your free time?　　*B:* I (　　　　) to watch movies.

Quick Search on the Web 🔍

The words or phrases below are closely related to universities in the U.S. What is each one? Do some quick searches and report to your group or class.

1. GPA　　**2.** Reading Days
3. How large are the stadiums at Michigan University and Ohio State University

---

B Use the expressions you learned in A. First, change your partner and ask the same five questions to your NEW partner. Then ask extra questions.

Example

A: How're you doing?

A: Pretty good. Thank you. May I ask your name?

A: I'm Masato. Takenokoshi Masato.

A: Yes. I hear there are only 70 people with this name in Japan.

A: What's your major?

B: Not bad. You?

B: I'm Yuka. .... and your name is?

B: That's an interesting last name.

B: Wow. Interesting.

B: Don't ask me. We're in the same department—communication.

C Interview each other. Make a group of three (or find a new partner). Ask these questions and one of your own. Take notes. Some hints are listed in [ ].

1. OK. I'm Reiko. May I ask your name? [My name is…. What's your name?]

2. Where did you go to high school? [I went to… in …..]

3. How did you like your high school?
[I loved it because… / Not so much because…]

4. What was your favorite and least favorite subject?
[I liked … best and I didn't like…much.]

5. Were you in any school clubs? [Yes. I was in the… / No.]

6. How do you come to school? [I take the train / take the bus / drive / walk.]

7. Was this school your first choice? [Yes. I'm really happy. / No, I wanted to go to…]

8. What do you want to do while in college? Anything special?
[Yes… / No, I just want to relax.]

9. What do you like best about this university?
[Teachers are nice / It's close to the station.]

10. (your own question) _____

For taking notes...

Interviewee's name 1 : (   )

Interviewee's name 2 : (   )

Magic "Hi"

If you need to ask a question, first say "Hi" while looking at your partner with a smile. Then ask the question. This magic "Hi" makes people listen to you more carefully and comfortably.

Example

Hi. (Smile and look at your partner.) My name is Naoya. Can I ask your name?

Smile and ask the following questions to your partner. Pair up and practice.

1. *(Smile)* Hi, how do you come to school?　　　　　　　　　[by bus / by train / on foot,…]

2. *(Smile)* Hi, how do you like this English class?　　　　　　　[I love it. / It's OK.…]

3. *(Smile)* Hi, where were you born?　　　　　　　　　　　　[I was born in ….]

Active Listening

 DL 05　　 CD1-05

Listen to Christen talk on LINE about her life in Japan to her father back in the U.S. Take notes and tell your partner about her life in Japan in the following areas.

1. new friends: _____

2. Japanese language: _____

3. food: _____

4. gaining weight: _____

5. something her father has to worry about: _____

Active Reading

 DL 06   CD1-06

Read the passage about some interesting facts about American universities.

Here are some interesting facts about some American colleges.

Universities in the U.S. excel in many areas, but their size is next to none. For example, the California
5 Community Colleges system has over 2,000,000 students. Eight universities have stadiums that hold over 100,000 people, double the size of Tokyo National Stadium. On the other hand, Japanese universities don't even have small stadiums. The number of books
10 that universities in the U.S. have is surprising, too. Harvard has the largest academic library in the world with 15.8 million volumes. Tokyo University has around 10 million books.

Some American universities are very unique as well. For example, Southampton College once invited Kermit the Frog - a muppet character from Sesame Street - to
15 their graduation ceremony. They even gave him an honorary doctorate degree. The University of Michigan-Ann Arbor has a Squirrel Club with over 400 members, but Japanese universities are just as unique when it comes to clubs. Among them are a Fusuma Club, Banzai Circle, Kakurenbo (hide-and-seek) Circle, Pokémon Lovers Club, etc. Can you name any other unique clubs at your school?

A Take turns reading the passage aloud to a partner and ask the questions below.

1. How many students does the California Community Colleges system have?
2. How large are some of the largest college stadiums in the U.S.?
3. Which university library has the most volumes of books in the world?
4. Who came to a graduation ceremony at Southampton College as a unique guest speaker?
5. Which club or circle mentioned above would you like to join? Why?

Quick Search on the Web

Search for information about the statement below. You can use your cellphone or laptop if allowed. Do this with your partner or in a group. Share answers with your classmates.

1. World famous college dropouts. Name at least two.
2. The number of books your university library has.
3. College tuition (and fees) for Harvard University and your school.

Activator
Open-ended Practice

A Find someone who answers "Yes" to your questions. Stand up and move around. Talk to as many people as possible. If someone answers "Yes," write down their name. Keep asking the same question until you find someone who says "Yes."

Example **Find someone who:**

comes to school on foot [Do you…?]
A: Do you come to school on foot?
B: Yes. I walk to school every day.
C: Good. May I have your name?

Someone who: **List of Names**

1. comes to school on foot [Do you come to…?]
(   )

2. went to high school in the countryside [Did you…?]
(   )

3. wants to work overseas in the future [Do you…?]
(   )

4. lives in an apartment [Do you…?] (   )

5. loves to sing at a karaoke box [Do you…?]
(   )

6. came to the open campus of this school [Did you…?]
(   )

7. has never been to Tokyo Disneyland [Have you ever…?]
(   )

B In a group of three or four, discuss the following statements. Do you agree or disagree? Give reasons and examples.

1. It's a waste of time and money to go to university.

2. School life in college is much more interesting and fun than it is in high school.

Future Plans / Jobs

Focus

Telling Intentions

⚡ Brainstorm

A Pair up and talk about yourself and your partner. Examples are shown in [   ].

1. *A:* What is really important to you in your life?

   B: _____.   [Money / Experiences / Happiness / My career]

2. *A:* What do you want to do in the future?

   B: I'm not sure, but I think I'd like to _____.

                        [be a teacher / work overseas]

3. *A:* At what age are you thinking of getting married?

   B: I'm planning to get married _____.   [by 28 / before I turn 35]

     (I'm not planning to get married.)

4. *A:* What is your ideal future partner like?

   B: They should be rich, gentle, and _____.

                           [good looking / outgoing]

B Switch roles. This time add one or two extra comments. See the example below. Go over 1-4 above again. Below is an example for exercise number one.

   A: What is really important to you in your life?

   B: Money, of course.

   A: What? Money cannot buy you love.

   B: Haha, but love cannot make you rich.

   A: OK. What else is important?

   B: ....

Dialogue

 DL 07   CD1-07

Hina is talking to Kevin, an international student, about her future job. Role-play the dialogue with your partner. Then switch roles and practice again.

Hina: Kevin, you know what? I think I've found my dream job.

Kevin: Really? What is it?

Hina: I'm going to be a YouTuber. I can work at home and make a lot of money.

Kevin: What? Are you serious?

Hina: ...Just kidding! Actually, I'd like to work for Yahoo Japan.

Kevin: That's good. That's a big IT company and you can use your computer skills.

Hina: Right. Now I have to work really hard to get into that company.

Kevin: Great idea.

A Ask at least two questions about the dialogue to your partner. Take turns.

B Replace the underlined parts with your own information and practice the conversation again. Be original and creative. Try to add a few more lines at the end.

C Listen to the rest of the conversation. Circle either True or False.

DL 08   CD1-08

1. Yahoo Japan sells Japanese manga overseas. — True / False

2. Kevin and Adam learned Japanese together in the U.S. — True / False

3. Adam is an IT engineer at Yahoo Japan. — True / False

4. Hina is busy translating manga into English. — True / False

5. Kevin likes Japanese manga very much. — True / False

16

Expressions 🎧 DL 09   💿 CD1-09

A Practice each dialogue with your partner.

1. *A:* What do you want to do in the future?
   B: I don't know, but **I'd like to be** <u>rich</u>.

2. *A:* **I want to work for** <u>an airline</u>.
   B: **Go for it**.

3. *A:* **What are your future plans**?
   B: First I'll try to find a <u>rich</u> partner and...

4. *A:* How many children would you like to have?
   B: **I'm thinking of** having <u>two</u> kids.

5. *A:* **What is your dream** honeymoon **like**?
   B: Well, I'd like to spend at least <u>two weeks</u> in <u>Hawaii</u>.

B Replace the underlined words with your own words and practice again.

 Interactive Practice

A Expand your vocabulary. Read the list of the jobs below aloud to your partner. Then choose one job you would love to have among the list below. Give reasons to your partner. Do the same for a job you would hate to do.

homemaker / police officer / firefighter / photojournalist / banker /
shop clerk / salesperson / business owner / YouTuber / real estate agent /
engineer / programmer / soccer player / movie producer /
insurance salesperson / international businessman

Example
A: I'd love to stay home and take care of my kids.
B: Oh? You don't want to have a job?
A: C'mon. Being a homemaker is a full-time job that requires a lot of skills and energy. Besides, I love cooking and playing with children.

Quick Search on the Web

What do they do? Search the term online with a partner.
1. Meteorologist **2.** Voice over artist **3.** Knocker-up

B Use the expressions below and show your intentions. Your partner needs to give a short comment. Follow the example.

> A: *I'd like to... / I'm thinking about... / I'm planning to...*
> B: *Go for it! / Way to go! / Great idea! / Are you serious? / That's not a good idea.*

Example

A: I'm thinking about buying a new car this summer.

B: <u>Good. Take me for a drive in your new car.</u>

1. A: ...work for Toyota Motor Corporation.

B: _____

2. A: ...find a nice partner and have at least two children.

B: _____

3. A: ...quitting my boring part-time job and finding another one.

B: _____

4. A: ...find a job in Australia and live there for the rest of my life.

B: _____

C Talk about your future plans for your next summer vacation and for when you turn thirty. Your partner needs to ask you how you can achieve those goals. Take turns.

Example

1. A: So, **what are you doing** next summer vacation?

B: **I'm thinking about** travelling all around Japan.

A: Wow. **That's a great idea.** Are you travelling alone?

B: No, I'll find somebody to travel with. ...You?

A: Me? Seriously? ...Yes, I'd love to do that.

B: Great! OK. Now we have to make some money first....

2. A: **How about** when you turn 30? **Any plans**?

B: Well, **by 30, I'd like to** be married and have at least one child.

A: Are you serious?

B: ...and **I want to** have my own house built in Tokyo.

A: That's a lot. How are you going to do all of that?

B: Let's see.... I will....

Communication **Strategy**

Fillers

Eeto, *Anoo* and *Sodesune* are all Japanese fillers. With these little words, you can save time and think about what you'd really like to say. In English you can say, "Well," "Let's see," "Let me think," or "How can I put it?" Practice saying them with a partner.

1. **A:** What kind of future partner would you like to find?
   B: Well, let's _____. I'd like to find a rich husband and....
2. **A:** If your grandfather left you 100 million yen, what would you do?
   B: Wow. Let me _____. I would....
3. **A:** What do we need to find a good job? Any idea?
   B: _____. I think communication skills are very important.

Active Listening

 DL 10   CD1-10

Listen and find out where they work. Choose the correct place they are working at from the list.

1. (   )   **2.** (   )   **3.** (   )   **4.** (   )

a. *Cram school*

b. *School library*

c. *Restaurant*

d. *Moving company*

Read the passage about two people who started a company with a very unique motto.

Some people keep working at a job they don't like because of money or other reasons. But some people quit their job because they've found something more important:

5 success and happiness. David and Mike Radparver are among them. They quit their jobs and founded a T-shirt company in New York in 2009. They wanted a company that would allow them to live their dreams. To start a company, they first wrote a company

10 motto. It's called the "Holstee Manifesto." They put it on their webpage. Then people around the world just loved it so much that it has been translated into over 14 languages. It starts like this:

"This is your life. Do what you want and do it often. If you don't like something, change it. If you don't like your job, quit. If you don't have enough time, stop

15 watching TV. ..."

You want to read more? Search for "Holstee Manifesto" on the net. It may change the way you think about success and your future.

A Take turns reading the passage aloud to a partner and ask the questions below.

1. Who started a T-shirt company in 2009?

2. Why did they start the company?

3. What's another word for "manifesto?" Find it in the passage.

4. What happened after they put the manifesto online?

5. According to this manifesto, what do you need to do if you don't like your job?

 Quick Search on the Web

Search for "Holstee Manifesto" and read it aloud to a partner. You can use your cellphone or laptop if allowed. Ask what they think about it or discuss in class.

Activator
Open-ended Practice

A Draw your dream house in the corner of a page in your notebook. Talk about it with a partner. Then, discuss your future dreams such as dream partner, dream job, dream trip, and others. Ask questions to each other. Ask each other questions below.

Example

A: What is your future dream house like?

B: Well, it has to be large. I need at least three bedrooms and two bathrooms.

A: OK. Do you want your own study or game room too?

B: Of course. ...and I need a basement and a large front yard. I can play with my kids and dog there on a sunny weekend. Doesn't that sound wonderful?

1. What is your dream partner like?
   -Does the person look like somebody famous?
   -Is the person good looking, rich, kind, and funny?
   -What else do you want from your dream partner?

2. What is the perfect future job for you?
   -How much do you want to make a year?
   -Would you like to be the president of a company? Why?
   -Do you want to work overseas for a while?

3. What is your dream trip/job like?

B In a group of three or four, discuss the following. If you could choose only one of the following, which one would you choose: a life with a high paying job that you love with a bad partner or a life with a low paying job that you hate, but you are with your dream partner?

Part-Time Jobs and Otakatsu

Focus

Talking about the Weekend

⚡ Brainstorm

A Pair up and talk about yourself and your partner. Examples are shown in [   ].

1. **A:** How was your weekend?

B: _____. [Excellent / not so good]

I stayed home and _____. [relaxed / did some homework]

2. **A:** What do you do on your day off?

B: Um, I'm usually busy with _____.

[Otakatsu / playing computer games]

3. **A:** Would you like to _____ this Saturday?

[go canoeing / have a barbecue]

B: _____.

[I'd love to / Sorry, I have another appointment]

4. **A:** I work part time at _____ on Saturday.

[a restaurant / Seven-Eleven]

B: How do you like your job?

B Switch roles. This time add one or two extra comments. See the example below. Go over 1-4 above again. Below is an example for exercise number two.

A: What do you do on your day off?

B: Um, I'm usually busy with Otakatsu.

A: <u>What's that?</u>

B: <u>Otaku activities. I follow Dogenzaka 26.</u>

A: <u>Oh my!</u>

 # Dialogue

Gerry and Haruka are talking about their weekend on Monday morning. Role-play the dialogue with your partner. Then switch roles and practice again.

Haruka: Did you have a good weekend?

Gerry: Yeah. I went <u>canoeing down the Kiso River</u>.

Haruka: That's great. Did you have a good time?

Gerry: I sure did. It was <u>an awesome</u> experience.

Haruka: I really envy you.

Gerry: Oh? You didn't have a good weekend?

Haruka: No, I just stayed home and <u>studied for the quiz</u>.

Gerry: Sorry to hear that. What is the quiz for?

Haruka: <u>Intro to Psychology</u>. You forgot?

Gerry: What? We have a quiz today?

A Ask at least two questions about the dialogue to your partner. Take turns.

B Replace the underlined parts with your own information and practice the conversation again. Be original and creative. Try to add a few more lines at the end.

C Listen to the rest of the conversation. Complete the summary by filling in the blanks with appropriate words listed below.

30	*sleeping*	*25*	*grade*	*kidding*	*cheat*	*prepare*

Gerry forgot that he had a quiz in his psychology class today and did not [1]( ) for it. The teacher told the class they'd have a quiz, but Gerry was [2]( ) in class last week. The quiz counts for [3]( ) % towards the final [4]( ), so he should not skip the quiz. Now he has to study for the quiz, but he has only [5]( ) minutes. He asked Haruka to sit next to him so that he could [6]( ), but Haruka, of course, refused. Gerry was just [7]( ).

 # Expressions

A Practice each dialogue with your partner.

1. *A:* **What are you doing this weekend?**
　　B: I'm <u>working part-time</u> the whole weekend.

2. *A:* **How was your weekend?**
　　B: <u>Just great</u>.

3. *A:* **Do you have any plans for** next weekend?
　　B: Yes, I'm going to <u>go out with Miki</u>.

4. *A:* **What do you do** at the restaurant?
　　B: I'm <u>a waiter and a cook</u>.

5. *A:* **How much do you make** an hour as a tutor?
　　B: I make <u>1,800 yen</u> an hour.

B Replace the underlined words with your own words and practice again. Be original and creative.

 # Interactive Practice

A Below are several ways to respond to "How was your weekend?" Fill in the blanks with one of the phrases listed below. Number 2 is done for you.

Just super	*Pretty good*	*Not bad*	*Not so good*	*Terrible*

A: How was your weekend?

B:
1. _____　　I lost my phone and I worked 12 hours straight.
2. __Pretty good__　　We saw a baseball game in Yokohama.
3. _____　　I got some good rest.
4. _____　　I just stayed home doing nothing.
5. _____　　I went to Tokyo Disneyland with Takuya.

🔍 **Quick Search on the Web**

What is the minimum wage per hour in your prefecture and in San Francisco? How about the average babysitting rates in some cities in the U.S.?

B Fill in the blanks with appropriate questions or answers listed below. Do this exercise orally with your partner.

> a. *Not really, but I can't complain. The pay is good.*
> b. *I don't have any plans. Why?*
> c. *You went to USJ? How did you like it?*
> d. *What can you teach?*
> e. *Did you have a good weekend?*

1. *A:* (   )   *B:* Couldn't have been better.

2. *A:* What are your plans for Saturday night?   *B:* (   )

3. *A:* Do you like your delivery work with Uber?   *B:* (   )

4. *A:* (   )   *B:* Not so great. It was too crowded.

5. *A:* I'd like to find a tutoring job.   *B:* (   )

C Talk about your ideal part-time job with your partner. Take turns asking the questions. First read the list of part-time jobs aloud. Do you know all these words?

> *cook / Uber Eats delivery person / gas station worker / teacher at a cram school / babysitter / model / telephone salesperson / construction worker / dog walker / manga assistant / teacher's assistant / university tour guide for high school students*

1. Do you mind working until late at night?

2. How much do you want to make an hour?

3. What kind of skills can you learn while working?

4. How about the flexibility of the hours?

5. How about the people you work with?

6. Would you prefer a low-paying easy job or a high-paying hard job?

7. So, what's the ideal part-time job you would like to get? Do you think you can get it?

8. Do you have a friend who has a great part-time job? What do they do?

Speak loudly

Speak loudly even if you're not confident or don't know the phrases you need. Surprisingly, your English will sound better, and people will understand you better that way. Pair up and stand up. Face each other and stand about two meters apart. Ask these questions and one of your own to your partner <u>as loudly as possible</u>. Your partner also needs to respond as loudly as possible. Add "How about you?" at the end. Begin.

1. *A:* Do you work part-time?
    B: Yes, I work at the Starbucks at the station. How about you?
2. *A:* How was your Golden Week this year?
    B: Pretty good. I had a barbecue. How about you?
3. *A:* What do you usually do on your dayoff?
    B: I sleep late and then work out after that. How about you?
4. *A:* (your original question) _____
    B: _____. How about you?

Active Listening   DL 15   CD1-15

Listen to Brian and Fuko talk about their favorite activities. Take notes and circle either True or False below.

1. The members of Baby Sitters are all female.   True / False

2. Fuko doesn't like heavy metal music.   True / False

3. Fuko travels to a place far away to see her favorite band.   True / False

4. Fuko gets tired from work and has no time for schoolwork.   True / False

5. Brian is making his own costume for the coming cosplay festival.   True / False

6. Fuko and Brian seem to like Otaku activities.   True / False

Active Reading 🎧 DL 16   ◎ CD1-16

The passage below is about the recently invented and widely used Japanese word "Otakatsu." Read the passage below.

New words are invented almost every day. Some are used for a while and forgotten, but some become recognized words or phrases. Among the recently recognized new Japanese words is "Otakatsu," a short

5 form for Otaku-Katsudo. Otakatsu (nerdy activities) is used to describe any kind of activities for those who are so crazy about pop idols or something that they follow them everywhere or collect anything related to them. Here are some other similar words that have "katsu" at the end of

10 the words.

1. "(-katsu)": Activities before going to work such as going to a gym, taking an English class, or joining a study group.

2. "(-katsu)": Single people's activities to look for a future husband or wife.

15 3. "(-katsu)": Job hunting activities for new graduates like writing resumes and visiting companies.

4. "(-katsu)": Activities towards the end of life; for example, making a will or getting rid of unnecessary things.

5. "(-katsu)": Seeing a doctor to get help becoming pregnant or

20 tracking body temperature.

A Pair up and your partner should close the textbook. Read the definition aloud to your partner. Your partner needs to tell you what word the definition is about.

⌈ Quick Search on the Web

Search for the information about the statement below. You could use your cellphone or laptop if allowed. Do this with your partner or in a group. Share answers with your classmates.

1. The difference between "geek" and "nerd." Both are translated as "Otaku" in Japanese.
2. The biggest comic convention (comicon) in the world. How many participants attend?

Activator
Open-ended Practice

A Plan a fun weekend. You have no homework to do, and you don't have to work part-time this weekend. What would you like to do with your partner? Some useful expressions are listed below.

> *go out to karaoke / dance at a club / go camping / go rafting / go to a baseball game / do some shopping / watch a movie / play soccer / go for a drive / go to a concert / play computer games / go canoeing / go to a comic convention / cosplay and walk around in Shibuya*

Example

1. *A:* OK. We have a totally free weekend. What do you want to do?
   B: Shall we <u>go for a drive to the Mt. Fuji area</u> on Saturday?
   A: Sounds good. But do you have a car? I don't.
   B: I don't, either. How about <u>going out to karaoke</u>?
   A: No, that's so boring. How about <u>(...ing)</u>＿＿＿＿＿＿＿?

2. *A:* We still have Sunday open. Do you want to ＿＿＿＿＿＿＿?
   B: No, no. I'd rather do something more exciting.
   A: How about ＿＿＿＿＿＿＿?
   B: Hey, that's a great idea. Let's do that.
   A: ...

B In a group of three or four, discuss the following statements. Do you agree or disagree? Give reasons and examples.

1. We all have to work for the rest of our life. We shouldn't work now if we don't have to.

2. We should do something more meaningful than Otakatsu. Otakatsu is a waste of time.

Unit 4 Movies

Focus

Inviting / Making Appointments

 Brainstorm

A Pair up and talk about yourself and your partner. Examples are shown in [ ].

1. *A:* What kind of movies do you like?
   B: I like _____. [action / comedy / romance / drama / sci-fi / horror]

2. *A:* What is the last movie you saw?
   B: Let me think. It was _____. [*Godzilla vs Spiderman*]

3. *A:* What's the best movie you've ever seen?
   B: It's _____. [*Princess Mononoke / Dead Poets Society*]

4. *A:* Would you like to go see a movie this weekend?
   B: _____. [With you? No way / Yes, I'd love to]

B Switch roles. This time add one or two extra comments. See the example below. Go over 1-4 above again. Below is an example for exercise number three.

   A: What's the best movie you've ever seen?
   B: It's *Coming to America*.
   A: <u>That's an old movie, isn't it?</u>
   B: <u>Yes, but it's a very funny comedy. It has some romance, too.</u>
   A: <u>Who plays the main character?</u>
   B: <u>Eddie Murphy. ...</u>

 # Dialogue

Russell is asking Ayami out for a movie. Role-play the dialogue with your partner. Then switch roles and practice again.

Russel: What are you doing this <u>Saturday</u>?

Ayami: Nothing special. Why?

Russel: Well, <u>*Godzilla vs Superman*</u> just came out. Would you like to go see it?

Ayami: Oh, I love those <u>*kaiju*</u> movies.

Russel: Great. So, you want to come?

Ayami: Sure. When and where?

Russel: How about <u>4:00 at the station</u>?

Ayami: <u>4:00 at the station</u> sounds good.

A Ask at least two questions about the dialogue to your partner. Take turns.

B Replace the underlined parts with your own information and practice the conversation again. Be original and creative. Try to add a few more lines at the end.

C Listen to the rest of the conversation. Circle either True or False.

1. They are meeting at the south gate of Yotsuya Station.   True / False

2. Ayami is working until 3:30 in Shinjuku on Saturday.   True / False

3. Movies usually start after 15 minutes of commercials.   True / False

4. They are meeting at 4:30 at Shinjuku Station.   True / False

5. The movie theater is probably in Shinjuku.   True / False

6. Ayami doesn't seem to think this is a date.   True / False

Expressions

 DL 19   CD1-19

A Practice each dialogue with your partner.

1. *A:* **Would you like to** see a movie <u>this weekend</u>?
   B: I'd love to. Thank you for asking.

2. *A:* **Do you want to join us for** <u>coffee after school</u>?
   B: Sure. Why not?

3. *A:* **I'm wondering if you might be interested in** <u>seeing a movie this Saturday</u>.
   B: Thanks, but I don't think I can. I've already got plans.

4. *A:* **How about** in front of <u>Cafeteria # 2 at 5:00</u>?
   B: <u>Cafeteria # 2 at 5:00</u>. Gotcha.

5. *A:* **Can I meet you** at <u>Starbucks around 6:00</u>?
   B: Can you make it <u>6:30</u>? I have to work till <u>5:00</u>.

B Replace the underlined words with your own words and practice again.

 # Interactive Practice

A Pair up and accept the invitations using the phrases below. Add one comment or question after accepting. Take turns. Number one is done for you.

I'd love to. / Thank you for asking. / Sure. Why not? / OK. When and where?

1. *A:* Are you interested in seeing a movie tonight?
   B: <u>I 'd love to. What are we seeing?</u>

2. *A:* Hey, you want to have lunch? I'm really hungry.
   B: _____

3. *A:* Why don't we play soccer this evening?
   B: _____

4. *A:* I was wondering if you'd like to have dinner with me?
   B: _____

5. *A:* Would you like to join us for coffee or something?
   B: _____

Quick Search on the Web 🔍

Find out which produces more movies, Hollywood in the U.S. or Bollywood in India? How many does each make in a year? How about in Japan?

B Pair up and refuse the invitation using the phrases below. Add a reason after refusing. Take turns. Number one is done for you.

> *I wish I could. / Sorry, I have another appointment. /*
> *I don't think I can. / I'm not interested.*

1. *A:* Would you like to barbeque this Saturday?

B: I wish I could. I have to work.

2. *A:* How would you like to see a movie with me?

B: _____

3. *A:* How about going for a drive this Saturday?

B: _____

4. *A:* We're having a party tonight. You want to come?

B: _____

C Invite your partner to the following events. Your partner should either accept or refuse the invitation. If you accept the invitation, decide when and where you are meeting. If you refuse the invitation, give reasons. Take turns.

Example

a gathering

A: Would you like to join us for a gathering this Saturday? Shota will be there.

B: That's great. Yeah, I'd love to get to know him better.

A: Great. I'll meet you at the school gate at five.

B: Five, at the gate. Got it. By the way, what kind of gathering is it?

A: Just drinking and some food.

B: OK. Food sounds good, but no drinking for me.

1. a movie
2. dinner at an Italian restaurant
3. class party this Saturday
4. karaoke and bowling
5. (your choice) _____

Assimilation

Some words are sometimes casually combined and sound totally different. This is called assimilation. This is the main reason why it's difficult to understand casual English. Practice them.

Example

Got you →Gotcha, call her →call'er, tell him →tell'im

1. I wanna (want to) go see *Wonder Woman Genesis*.
2. I'm gonna (going to) see *Avatar Next* this Friday.
3. I'll meetcha (meet you) at Umeda station at 6:30.
4. Could you tell'im (tell him) I'll be late?
5. Let's go see a monster movie, whatchamacallit (what you may call it?), in Japanese. Yes, Kaiju. Kaiju movie.

Active Listening

 DL 20 CD1-20

Listen to Katie and Taichi talking about movies. Take notes and write down the kind of movies they are talking about. Are they romance, horror, comedy, science fiction, action, fantasy, or drama?

No. 1 _____

No. 2 _____

No. 3 _____

Active Reading

Below is an essay about why we should watch movies at a theater, not at home. Pair up with your partner and take turns reading each paragraph aloud.

Do you prefer to watch movies at home or at a theater? Here are three reasons why you should watch movies at a theater.

The biggest reason is the big screen and massive
5 speaker system. You get pulled into the sound and images in a way that you don't feel when you're sitting on your couch at home.

The second reason is that you can focus on the movie more at the theater than at home. There are no distractions such as your family members, phones, or pets.
10 You also watch the movies more intensely than you do at home.

The third reason is that going to the movie theater is a special event. Going to the movies with someone you're dating can be a cherished memory. You buy popcorn and soda, watch the movie, get excited, and talk about it after the movie. It's almost like taking a short trip with someone special.

15 It seems that the "magic of the movies" really exists. Try going to the movies. You may fall in love with this experience.

A What are the three reasons why we should watch movies at a theater rather than at home? Give examples.

Reason 1: _____

Reason 2: _____

Reason 3: _____

Quick Search on the Web 🔍

Search for information about the questions below. You could use your cellphone or laptop if allowed. Do this with your partner or in a group. Share answers with your classmates.

1. How often do Americans and Japanese people go to the movies?
2. What is the average ticket price at U.S. movie theaters? How about in India?

Activator
Open-ended Practice

A Find a different partner and take turns asking and answering the questions below.

1. What's the best movie you have ever seen?

2. How often do you go to the movies?   [once a month / once a year / rarely]

3. Who is your favorite actor or actress? Why?

4. What do you think of...?   [the name of your favorite movie]

5. What is your favorite kind of movie?   [romance / comedy / drama / action]

6. Which do you prefer for a date, going to a movie or going for a drive? Why?

7. What is the last movie you went to? How did you like it?

8. Tell me more about it.

9. Would you like to go see a movie with me this weekend?

10. (your original question) _____

B In a group of three or four, discuss the following statements. Do you agree or disagree? Give reasons and examples.

1. Going to a movie is a waste of time. We should do something more active.

2. Disney animated movies are better than Japanese anime.

Parties and Festivals

Focus

Asking a Favor

⚡ Brainstorm

A Pair up and talk about yourself and your partner. Examples are shown in [   ].

1. *A:* Do you like to go to parties and festivals?
  B: Yes, I do. / No, I don't because _____.

[They're fun / I don't like noisy places]

2. *A:* What kind of parties do you like best?
  B: I like _____ parties.   [drinking / class / pajama]

3. *A:* Do you like cookouts?
  B: Yes. / No, because _____.   [I love to barbecue / I don't like bugs]

4. *A:* Could you name your favorite festival in your area?
  B: I love _____. [the Tone River Fireworks Festival / the local shrine festival]

B Switch roles. This time add one or two extra comments. See the example below. Go over 1-4 above again. Below is an example for exercise number one.

  A: Do you like to go to parties and festivals?
  B: Yes, I do because they're fun.
  A: What's your favorite kind of party?
  B: I like any kind. Talking with somebody I like is always fun.

 # Dialogue

DL 22 CD1-22

Ryota is talking to Jimari about the cookout this Saturday. Role-play the dialogue with your partner. Then switch roles and practice again.

Ryota: Jimari, could you bring a knife and a cutting board?

Jimari: What are you talking about?

Ryota: Sorry, about the cookout this Saturday.

Jimari: Ah, right. No problem. Anything else?

Ryota: No, but do you mind paying 3,000 yen in advance? We need to get some meat and vegetables.

Jimari: Sure. Can I give it to you tomorrow? I don't have that much now.

Ryota: Tomorrow is fine. No hurry.

Jimari: Thank you.

A Ask at least two questions about the dialogue to your partner. Take turns.

B Replace the underlined parts with your own information and practice the conversation again. Be original and creative. Try to add a few more lines at the end.

C Listen to the rest of the conversation. Complete the summary by filling in the blanks with appropriate words listed below. There are two unused words.

DL 23 CD1-23

umbrella tent father outdoor Momoka grill easier brother

Ryota asked Jimari if she has a ¹(   ) in case it rains, but she doesn't have one, so Jimari will ask ²(   ) if she has one. Ryota also needs a barbecue ³(   ). Jimari thinks Momoka has one because her father likes ⁴(   ) activities. They also need a car. Ryota said he can ask his ⁵(   ) to lend it to him, but Jimari thinks it's ⁶(   ) to ask Momoka's father to come along with them.

 # Expressions

A Practice each dialogue with your partner.

1. *A:* **Could you** bring <u>a knife and cutting board</u>?
   B: Sure. No problem.

2. *A:* **Will you do me a favor?**
   B: I <u>guess so</u>. What is it?

3. *A:* **Would you mind** pay**ing** <u>3,000 yen</u> in advance?
   B: Sorry, I don't think I can. <u>I'm broke</u> now.

4. *A:* **Could I have** another <u>soft drink</u>?
   B: Which would you like, <u>Coke or Seven-up</u>?

5. *A:* **Can I ask** your name?
   B: Sure. My name is Suzuki <u>Hina</u>. Please call me <u>Hina.</u>

B Replace the underlined words with your own words and practice again. Be original and creative.

 # Interactive Practice

A What kind of parties are they? Fill in the blanks.

housewarming *farewell* *potluck* *surprise* *baby shower*

1. A _____ party is not made known beforehand to the person it's for.

2. You have to bring a cooked dish or some drinks to a _____ .

3. If you're leaving a job, your co-workers might throw you a _____ party.

4. At a _____ , a couple having a baby receives many gifts.

5. A couple may hold a _____ party when they start living in a new house.

Quick Search on the Web 🔍

Find out what a "bachelor party" is? How about a prom? What happens at these parties?

B Learn some expressions you may use at parties. Imagine you're at a party. What expressions would you use in the situations below? Draw a line while you orally practice with your partner.

1. You meet the host at the entrance. · · Will you do me a favor?
2. You have a favor to ask. · · Can I have some water please?
3. You want to get to know somebody. · · I don't think we've met before.
4. You want something to drink. · · Oh, you didn't have to. Thank you.
5. You want to say nice things about · · Thank you for inviting us.
   the party.
6. You want to help someone to get · · What can I get you, Hibiki?
   some drinks.
7. Somebody brought you a nice gift. · · This is a really nice party.

C What would you say in the situations below. Use the expressions below. Your partner needs to either accept the favor or refuse it. Add one extra comment or reason. Number one is done for you.

Asking favors	Responses
Could you...? *Would you mind...ing...?* *Can I ask you to...?*	*Sure, I'd be happy to.* *No problem.* *No, I don't mind.*
	Sorry, I can't. I... *I wish I could, but I...* *No way.*

1. **You want your senpai to bring some wine to the party.**
   A: Senpai, can I ask you to bring some wine to the party tonight?
   B: Sure. I'd be happy to. Anything else?
   A: Well, could you also chip in 10,000 yen?
   B: Ha-ha. Nice try. Sorry.

2. You're too tired. You want your friend to drive you home.
3. You forgot your wallet today. You want your partner to pay for your lunch.
4. You have no alarm clock. You want your roommate to wake you up tomorrow at 6:00.
5. Your teacher is speaking too fast. You want them to slow down a bit.

Be polite

It's very important to be polite when you ask for a favor. Use "could" or "would" instead of "can" or "will" and add a "please" to the end of the sentence. How can you make the sentences below more polite? Pair up and practice with your partner. Your partner needs to respond.

Example

Hey, pass me the salt.

A: Could you pass me the salt, please?

B: Sure. Here it is.

1. I want a menu. Also, give me water.
2. I need a receipt for this.
3. What's your name?
4. Give us a ride to the campsite on Saturday.

Active Listening

 DL 25   CD1-25

A Listen to three sets of conversations. What kind of parties are they planning?

No. 1 _____

No. 2 _____

No. 3 _____

Active Reading

 DL 26   CD1-26

Below is a passage about *hibachi* in the U.S. Take turns reading each paragraph aloud with your partner.

Americans love to barbecue. They often invite people to their house and have a cookout. They all seem to have at least one large barbecue grill at home. They usually call it a barbecue, but did you know that small barbecues
5 are sometimes called *hibachi* in the U.S.?

A *hibachi* is a traditional Japanese open-topped heating bowl that holds charcoal. However, in the U.S., *hibachi* means a portable barbecue grill. You can buy one at any DIY store. *Hibachi* is also the name of a kind of Japanese
10 *teppanyaki* restaurant. So, some Americans think that a *hibachi* is a large flat metal plate where a chef performs the cooking in front of the diners.

There are some other imported Japanese words that are very commonly used in the U.S. Among them are, *bonsai, futon, panko, shiitake, bento, dashi, anime,*
15 *otaku, cosplay, origami, kawaii, ninja, sudoku,* and *karaoke*. What other words would you like to export to American English?

A Ask the questions below to your partner. If your partner responds correctly, repeat the answer. If wrong, give your partner a correct answer.

1. What is another name for a barbecue grill?
2. What do some Americans call a small barbecue grill?
3. Where can you buy a small barbecue grill in the U.S.?
4. What does *hibachi* mean to Americans besides a small barbecue grill?
5. Which Japanese words used in English that are listed are the most surprising to you and why?

Quick Search on the Web

Search for any other Japanese words exported into English. Which one do you find most interesting?

1. Other Japanese words:
2. Which one is interesting and why?

Activator
Open-ended Practice

A Move around and find someone who has done the following activities. If a person answers "yes," then write down that person's name. Be sure to ask follow-up questions such as "How was it?" "Are you serious?" or "Tell me more about it."

Example **Find someone who:**

Have you been to...? May I have your name?

Someone who: **List of Names**

1. has been to a birthday party in the last three years

(   )

2. prefers playing games at home to going to parties

(   )

3. has missed the train or a bus because of a party

(   )

4. has been to a party with non-Japanese people

(   )

5. has hosted a party

(   )

6. wants to have a class party before summer

(   )

7. loves to have a barbecue

(   )

B Plan some kind of party or a barbecue with your classmates and your teacher. Make sure to discuss:

1. What kind of party is it? (drinking, dinner, barbecue, potluck, dance, karaoke...)
2. Where and what time do you want to hold the party or barbecue?
3. How much do people need to chip in?
4. Who should be the host?
5. If it's a potluck party, what would you bring?

Unit 6 — Friends

Focus

Appreciating / Apologizing

 ## Brainstorm

A Pair up and talk about yourself and your partner. Examples are shown in [ ].

1. *A:* Do you have any international friends?
   B: _____.

[Yes, I have some / No, but I'd like to make some]

2. *A:* How did you meet your best friend?
   B: _____.

[I met them in the Kendo club / They are my neighbor]

3. *A:* Who do you usually hang out with after school or on weekends?
   B: Let's see. I hang out with _____.

[my high school friends / my boyfriend or girlfriend]

4. *A:* Have you ever done anything bad to your best friend?
   B: Yes, I _____.

[told them a big lie / stole their lunch]

B Switch roles. This time add one or two extra comments. See the example below. Go over 1-4 above again. Below is an example for exercise number one.

   A: Do you have any international friends?
   B: Yes, I have some.
   A: <u>Oh, how did you meet them?</u>
   B: <u>I met them in the cafeteria. I helped them buy tickets for lunch.</u>
   A: <u>Oh, that's nice.</u>

43

Dialogue

Moeka is apologizing to Chris for having called him "gaijin." Role-play the dialogue with your partner. Then switch roles and practice again.

Moeka: I'm really sorry about <u>yesterday</u>. I didn't mean to hurt you.

Chris: I know you didn't mean to, but it still hurt me.

Moeka: I'll never call you a *gaijin* again.

Chris: Please don't because I'm not a *gaijin*. I'm <u>American</u> and your <u>boyfriend</u>... aren't I?

Moeka: Yes, sorry. I apologize. I really mean it.

Chris: I hope you understand.

Moeka: I do, <u>Chris</u>. I'm sorry again.

A Ask at least two questions about the dialogue to your partner. Take turns.

B Replace the underlined parts with your own information and practice the conversation again. Be original and creative. Try to add a few more lines at the end.

C Listen to the rest of the conversation. Circle either True or False.

1. Chris accepted Moeka's apology.   True / False

2. Moeka does not want to tell people that she is dating Chris.   True / False

3. Moeka will probably introduce Chris as her boyfriend now.   True / False

4. Chris thinks that people will soon find out that they are dating.   True / False

5. Moeka thinks that Chris should be more open with her.   True / False

Expressions

🎧 DL 29   ◎ CD1-29

A Practice each dialogue with your partner.

1. *A:* **Thank you so much for** <u>inviting me</u>.
   B: You're quite welcome.

2. *A:* **I really appreciate** <u>your help</u>.
   B: No problem.

3. *A:* **I'm terribly sorry.** I didn't mean to <u>hurt you</u>.
   B: <u>That's all right</u>.

4. *A:* **I apologize for** <u>the mistake</u>.
   B: No need to apologize. It was my fault.

5. *A:* You look so <u>sharp</u> in that suit.
   B: Really? **It's so nice of you to say that.**

B Replace the underlined words with your own words and practice again. Be original and creative.

 Interactive Practice

A Group the phrases below into three categories.

Sorry to bother you. / My pleasure. / I don't know how I can thank you enough. / That's all right. / Not at all. / I apologize. / Excuse me. / I really appreciate it. / Sure. / That's very kind of you.

Apologizing	Appreciating	Accepting

Quick Search on the Web

How many different gestures can you find for appreciation and apologizing around the world? Report them to the group or class.

B Respond to the statements below with your own answer. Make <u>two</u> statements like those in example. Do this orally first and then write down your response.

> **Example**
>
> *A:* It's very kind of you to give me a ride to school this morning.
>
> *B:* (1) No problem. (2)...if you buy me lunch today. Just kidding.

1. *A:* I'm sorry I'm late. I promise I'll never be late again.

   B: _____

2. *A:* Why didn't you call me last night? I was waiting for your call.

   B: _____

3. *A:* Thank you so much for showing me around town.

   B: _____

4. *A:* You promised to show up, but you didn't. What happened?

   B: _____

C Complete the dialogue with the expressions of either appreciation or acceptance such as "Thank you," "No problem," "Don't worry," or any other similar expressions and role-play the dialogue. Then role-play the dialogue again by replacing the underlined parts with your own information. <u>Add a few more lines at the end</u>. Be original and creative.

Hiro: _____ so much for showing me around <u>Kyoto</u>. I had a really good time.

Yuna: _____. I had fun too.

Hiro: It's very kind of you to <u>take a day off</u> for me. Hope your boss won't be too angry.

Yuna: _____. I told him I had to <u>attend a funeral for a relative</u>.

Hiro: Oh, no. You said that?

Yuna: Yeah. But don't worry. He didn't seem to care.

Hiro: _____, <u>Yuna</u>. ...Oh, by the way, did you have time to <u>make a hotel reservation</u> for me?

Yuna: Oh, I completely forgot. How stupid of me. I'm terribly <u>sorry</u>, <u>Hiro</u>. I'll do it right now.

Hiro: _____. We can do that later. Let's have <u>dinner</u> first. I'm so hungry.

Yuna: _____

Hiro: _____

Communication   Strategy

Inserting names

Insert the name of the person you are talking to in your conversations from time to time. He or she will understand that you are trying to be friendly, and your message will have stronger impact. Role-play the dialogue below once. Then, change the underlined parts and practice again.

Keisuke: Thank you very much, <u>Megumi</u>.

Megumi: You don't need to thank me. <u>Keisuke</u>, you did most of the work.

Keisuke: Well, still. Let me buy you <u>lunch</u> today. I really want to.

Megumi: Don't worry, <u>Keisuke</u>. But... I'll accept <u>ice cream</u>, though.

Keisuke: <u>Ice cream</u> is fine with me. I love <u>ice cream</u>.

Active Listening

 DL 30   CD1-30

Important words are stressed more strongly than other words. Underline the words that are strongly stressed first. Then listen to the recording and see if you answered correctly. Finally, role-play the dialogue with your partner.

Example

A: I don't know how I can thank you enough. I really appreciate your help.
B: I have to thank <u>you</u>. <u>You</u> helped me a lot with the project.

1. A: I really appreciate your hospitality. I had a very good time in Kobe.
   B: No, no. Please thank Kenta, not me. He arranged the whole thing.

2. A: Rinka, I was waiting for you here for almost 30 minutes. What happened?
   B: Oh, I'm terribly sorry. I thought we were meeting at the station, not here.

3. A: I owe you an apology, Tomoki.
   B: Don't apologize. It was my fault. I should have told you earlier.

4. A: So, you don't like Japanese food.
   B: Don't get me wrong. I do like Japanese food. I just don't like *natto*.

Active Reading

Can men and women be "just friends?" Here are the findings of a research paper. [*]

Can men and women be "just friends?" Researchers at the University of Wisconsin asked female and male "friends" what they really think and got very different answers. They asked 88 pairs of undergraduate opposite-sex friends a series of questions. They found that men were much more attracted to their female friends
5   than women were to their male friends. Men were also more likely than women to think that their opposite-sex friends were attracted to them—a clearly misguided belief.

Also, 249 adults were asked to list the positive and negative aspects of being friends with the opposite sex. The results showed that males were five times more
10   likely than females to list romantic attraction, such as "our relationship could lead to romantic feelings" as a benefit of opposite-sex friendships.

The study suggests that women seem to believe that opposite-sex friendships are quite possible, but men tend to not let go of their hope for something more. It seems that men, relative to women, have a particularly hard time being "just
15   friends."

A Ask the questions below to your partner. If your partner responds correctly, repeat the answer. If they respond incorrectly, give your partner the correct answer.

1. Where did this research take place?
2. What did the researchers find out by asking 88 pairs of college students?
3. How many people were asked to list the positive and negative aspects of being friends with the opposite sex?
4. Who listed romantic attraction as a benefit of opposite-sex friendships more, males or females?
5. Who has a more difficult time being just friends, men or women?

Quick Search on the Web

Search for "how to make friends" or "tips to make friends." There are so many ways listed. Which one do you agree with most? Which one is the most unique? Share your thoughts with your partner or the class.

1. Agree with most:
2. Most unique:

---

[*](April Bleske-Rechek et.al (2012) Benefit or burden? Attraction in cross-sex friendship, *Journal of Social and Personal Relationships* 459-596, DOI: 10.1177/0265407512443611)

Activator
Open-ended Practice

A This is a game to play against your partner. You need to keep asking questions to your partner about his or her closest friend(s) and your partner needs to keep answering questions. If someone stays quiet for more than five seconds, that person loses. Change partners and repeat the game several times.

Sample Questions:

1. Who is/are your best friend(s)?

2. How did you meet him/her/them?

3. How long have you been close to each other?

4. Tell me good things about him/her/them.

5. Can you talk about anything with him/her/them?

6. Have you ever done anything stupid with your closest friend(s)?

7. Tell me more about it.

8. Do you have any close friend(s) of the opposite sex?

9. What do you think about having friends of the opposite sex?

10. (your original question) _____

11. (your original question) _____

B Try to make new friends in this class. Stand and line up facing somebody you don't know well. Ask several questions about your partner for about a few minutes. Say "Nice meeting you" at the end of the conversation. Then move two steps to your left. Now you're facing somebody new. Repeat the same process until you make several new friends.

Focus

Asking for Repetition

Brainstorm

A Pair up and talk about yourself and your partner. Examples are shown in [ ].

1. *A:* Would you like to study abroad while you're in college?

   B: _____. [Yes, of course / No, I'm happy staying in Japan]

2. *A:* Where would you like to go?

   B: _____. [I'd like to go to Australia / I'd like to go to the U.S.]

3. *A:* Which program would you prefer, a short summer program or a year-long program?

   B: Let's see. _____. [I'd prefer a short program / The longer, the better]

4. *A:* Is the Philippines a good choice for studying English abroad? Why or why not?

   B: _____. [Yes, it's close to Japan / No, their accent is too strong]

B Switch roles. This time add one or two extra comments. See the example below. Go over 1-4 above again. Below is an example for exercise number one.

   A: Would you like to study abroad while you're in college?
   B: Yes, but I don't think my English is good enough.
   A: <u>That's why we should study abroad.</u>
   B: <u>Do you think they can understand my English?</u>
   A: <u>Well, you'll find out if you go.</u>

Dialogue

DL 32   CD1-32

Shunya is studying English in the U.S. He is talking to his friend Jessica. Role-play the dialogue with your partner. Then switch roles and practice again.

Shunya: You know what?

Jessica: What?

Shunya: I'm here in the U.S., but I'm listening to <u>Korean</u> English more than American English.

Jessica: What do you mean by that?

Shunya: Well, I've made a lot of <u>Korean</u> friends here, and I'm talking to them all the time.

Jessica: Well, at least you're speaking English. That's good.

Shunya: True. I also met a <u>Singlish</u> speaker yesterday.

Jessica: What? Can you say that again?

Shunya: I said I met a <u>Singlish</u> speaker. You know, a <u>Singaporean</u> who speaks <u>Singapore English</u>.

Jessica: Ah, got it.

A Ask at least two questions about the dialogue to your partner. Take turns.

B Replace the underlined parts with your own information and practice the conversation again. Be original and creative. Try to add a few more lines at the end.

C Listen to the rest of the conversation and answer the questions.

DL 33   CD1-33

1. Does Shunya like Singlish? Why or why not?

2. Does Jessica have any problem understanding Shunya's English?

3. Why is Shunya happy to be in the U.S.?

4. What kind of English is Shunya particularly interested in hearing?

5. What are they going to do for lunch today?

 # Expressions

A Practice each dialogue with your partner.

1. **A: Sorry, can you say that again please?**
   B: Sure. I said I'm going to study English in India.

2. **A: I beg your pardon?**
   B: I said Singlish — a unique English spoken in Singapore.

3. **A: Could you slow down a bit?**
   B: Oh, I'm sorry. Of course.

4. *A:* My roommate is from Guatemala.
   B: Sorry, your roommate is **from where?**

5. **A: What do you mean by** "a Global English?"
   B: It means English that people all over the world find easy to understand.

B Replace the underlined words with your own words and practice again. Be original and creative.

 # Interactive Practice

A Fill in the blanks. Practice with your partner.

1. *A:* I met someone called Jimari Yacuzzo Oomameuda.
   B: You met (　　　　　　)?

2. *A:* (　　　　　　) me, but can you say that again?
   B: Sure, I (　　　　) we should join the online study abroad program.

3. *A:* What do you mean (　　　　　　) being trilingual.
   B: It means they speak three languages.

4. *A:* I (　　　　　) your pardon?
   B: I said we have a quiz in Dr. Martinelli's class.

5. *A:* Can you (　　　　　) the last word?
   B: Sure, it's TOEFL, the T-O-E-F-L test.

Quick Search on the Web 🔍

Find a website where you can listen to Singlish online. Try to find some unique features of Singlish and report them to your group or class.

B Your partner speaks too fast. Ask them to slow down. Use the expressions below. Your partner starts by reading sentences 1-5 below as fast as possible. You need to stop them and ask them to repeat.

> *You're speaking too fast. / Wait. Can you slow down a bit? /*
> *Stop. Can you repeat that, please? /*
> *Sorry, I couldn't follow you. / Would you mind speaking a bit more slowly?*

Your partner

1. Do you want to join this summer study abroad program in Indiana? What do you think?
2. Guess what? I can go to the University of New England next year.
3. Did you hear everybody can get a 100,000 yen scholarship if they join this study abroad program?
4. Did I tell you that I finally saved up one million yen to do an internship in Canada?
5. You know what? I got selected as an exchange student to the University of Illinois.

C What would you say in the situations below? Try to find a good phrase to ask for repetition from your partner. Your partner needs to respond to your request.

Example

You don't know how to pronounce "Micronesia."

A: Excuse me. How do you pronounce this word?
B: It's pronounced "My-kro-ni-jya."

1. You don't understand the expression "What's up?"
   A: Excuse me. What does "What's up?" mean?
   B: Well, it means _____.
2. You couldn't catch the first word "yummy" that your partner said?
   A: _____.
   B: _____.
3. Your partner is speaking too fast.
   A: _____.
   B: _____.
4. Your partner said, "I'll quit this school and go to Bhutan."
   A: _____.
   B: _____.
5. Your partner said, "Guess what? I've got an American boyfriend/girlfriend."
   A: _____.
   B: _____.

International English, please.

Add "International English, please." or "Can you say that again in plain English? This is another way of asking for repetition. Practice with your partner.

1. **A:** My English teacher hit the ceiling.
   B: _____
   A: Sorry, it means he got really angry.

2. **A:** That's a catch-22.
   B: _____
   A: Sorry, it means it's an impossible decision or there is no way out.

3. **A:** Pull over the car.
   B: _____
   A: Sorry, you have to stop the car at the side of the road.

Active Listening

 DL 35   CD1-35

Listen to the conversation between Sakura and Adam. If you think Adam agrees with the statements below, circle Agree, if not, circle Disagree.

1. Having an accent is OK if people understand.   Agree / Disagree

2. We don't have to get rid of our accent if people understand us.   Agree / Disagree

3. We should try to speak like a native speaker of English.   Agree / Disagree

4. A Japanese person could become an English teacher in America
   if they speak English well.   Agree / Disagree

5. Adam is not interested in meeting Wahab, a Nigerian student.   Agree / Disagree

Active Reading

DL 36   CD1-36

Here is a speech from a study abroad advisor on why you should study abroad. Act it out as if you were the study abroad advisor and your partner has come to a meeting to hear you speak about studying abroad.

Why should you study overseas? Well, obviously you could improve your foreign language skills but remember just breathing the air in a foreign country will not improve your foreign
5   language skills. You have to use the language.

The second reason is that the way you see things will change. For example, in the U.S., teachers wear jeans and bring coffee to their classrooms. They can be very casual. Students raise their hands all the time, study
10   seriously on weekdays, and have crazy parties on weekends. The way they do things is so different from Japan that you may realize that your way is not the only way to do things.

The third reason is the most important one. You'll become more mature and independent because you have to support yourself, solve your own problems, make
15   friends, and study hard. Then you will grow greatly and become a more internationally-minded, mature adult in a short period of time.

Studying overseas might cost you money and take a lot of energy, but believe me, it's worth doing it. It's a life changing experience.

A Summarize three reasons why you should study overseas according to the speech.

Reason 1: _____

Reason 2: _____

Reason 3: _____

Quick Search on the Web 🔍

Go to the website of the international office of your school. Find out what kinds of study abroad programs there are, how much they cost, and what conditions you have to meet to join the program. Then, discuss which one you might like to join and why.

1. Programs: _____
2. Costs: _____
3. Conditions: _____
4. Program you want to join: _____

Activator
Open-ended Practice

A Find a <u>new</u> partner and ask the following questions. Your partner should answer your questions and give reasons as well. Switch roles. Take notes.

1. If you had a chance to study abroad, where would you like to go? Why?

2. Would you like to join a school program, or would you rather go alone? Why?

3. What are some benefits of studying abroad?

4. What might be some of your biggest problems if you were to study abroad now? Are they language, money, culture stress, parents, job hunting, relationships, etc.?

5. Are countries like the Philippines, Hong Kong, India, Singapore, and Malaysia possible choices for studying abroad for you? They all have many English speakers and the cost is very low. Why or why not?

6. Would you mind living overseas for a long time? Why or why not?

7. Would you bring your whole family (your partner and children) if your company asked you to work overseas for five years? Why or why not?

B Do you agree or disagree with the statement below? In a group of three or four, discuss your opinions.

"If you seriously want to learn a foreign language, you should go to a country where the target language is spoken for at least a year or so."

SNS / Fashion / Weather

Focus

Expressions for Small Talk

⚡ Brainstorm

A Pair up and talk about yourself and your partner. Examples are shown in [　].

1. **A:** How often do you watch videos on YouTube?
    B: I watch them _____.　　[almost every day / once a while]

2. **A:** If you were in an elevator with your teacher, would you make small talk or stay quiet?
    B: I usually _____.　　[stay quiet / talk about the weather]

3. **A:** If there was nothing special to talk about, what would you talk about?
    B: I would talk about _____.
    [fashion / TV programs / music / Korean pop idols]

4. **A:** If you could start a YouTube channel, what would it be about?
    B: It'd be about _____.　　[club activities / my daily life / my bentos]

B Switch roles. This time add one or two extra comments. See the example below. Go over 1-4 above again. Below is an example for exercise number one.

A: How often do you watch videos on YouTube?
B: I watch them almost every day.
A: Really? What do you watch?
B: Mostly videos about my favorite singers. How about you?
A: I watch dance videos. You know I'm in the dance club.

57

Dialogue

Mone happens to be on the same train to school as a friend of hers from the international language exchange club. They started to make small talk. Role-play the dialogue with your partner. Then switch roles and practice again.

David: Hi, <u>Mone</u>. Another hot day, isn't it?

Mone: Oh, hi, <u>David</u>. Yes, it is. I can't stand this <u>humid</u> weather.

David: Me, neither. I can't wait for summer vacation.

Mone: Right. I don't feel like studying in this weather.

David: Yep... Hey, I like your <u>T-shirt</u>.

Mone: Thank you. I got this at a <u>flea market</u> for <u>only 500 yen</u>.

David: That's a good deal. What do those Kanji say?

Mone: *Yaju*.

David: What does that mean?

Mone: It means <u>I'm a beast</u>.

David: What?

A Ask at least two questions about the dialogue to your partner. Take turns.

B Replace the underlined parts with your own information and practice the conversation again. Be original and creative. Try to add a few more lines at the end.

C Listen to the rest of the conversation and complete the summary by filling in the blanks with appropriate words listed below.   DL 38   CD1-38

meant	*beauty*	*funny*	*kanji*	*Beast*	*train*

   Mone and David happened to be on the same ¹(   ). It was a hot and humid day. David saw Mone's T-shirt , which had a ²(   ) word— Yaju. David didn't know what it ³(   ), so he asked her. She said it means "beast". She likes it because she likes the Disney movie, Beauty and the ⁴(   ). David asked if there was also the kanji character for Beauty on her T-shirt. Mone answered it's not there but there is a ⁵(   ) right in front of David. He thought Mone was rather ⁶(   ).

58

Expressions

A Practice each dialogue with your partner.

1. *A:* **Did you watch** the game between Japan and England **last night**?
   B: Yes, <u>online</u>. It was so <u>exciting</u>, wasn't it?

2. *A:* **I like your** <u>T-shirt</u>. Where did you get it?
   B: Thank you. I got it at <u>UNIQLO</u> for <u>1,900</u> yen.

3. *A:* **Nice day, isn't it?**
   B: You think so? But it's another <u>cloudy</u> day.

4. *A:* **I hear** you started your own YouTube channel.
   B: Yes, I decided to upload <u>my own new songs</u> once a week.

5. *A:* **Hey, what's up**, <u>Satoshi</u>?
   B: **Not much.** How about you?

B Replace the underlined words with your own words and practice again. Be original and creative.

 # Interactive Practice

A Complete the word map with the words below.

| humid | fair | chilly | sunny | mild | snowy |
| wet | calm | stormy | muggy | freezing | showering |

hot	nice	cold	rainy

Quick Search on the Web

Try to find unique kanji words on a T-shirt that a non-Japanese person is wearing. Which one do you find the funniest? (key words: strange, kanji, T-shirt)

B Find an appropriate response. Practice with your partner.

A:

1. Did you watch the Giants game last night?

2. Hey, what's up, Yuta?

3. I like your hair style.

4. I heard you started a YouTube channel.

5. How do you like this weather?

B:

· *It's OK. I like rain.*

· *Thank you. I like it, too.*

· *Yes, wasn't it exciting? They won the title.*

· *Yes, it's about my lunch boxes.*

· *Not much. You?*

C Sometimes you can't find anything special you want to talk about. Well, then why don't you talk about the weather, fashion, YouTube channels, etc.? Ask the following questions to your partner. Your partner also needs to ask the questions back.

Weather

1. What's the weather like for tomorrow?   [I think it's going to be...]

2. Do you check the weather forecast every day?   [Yes, on an app on my phone... / No,...]

3. Do you like this weather?   [Yeah, I like it because...]

Fashion

1. How do you like my hair style/new watch?   [I think it's....]

2. You have a nice pair of sneakers/shoes.   [Thank you. I got them at....]

3. You seem to like casual fashion/big name brands.   [You think so? Actually,...]

YouTube

1. My little brother said he'd like to be a YouTuber.   [Funny, I was also...]

2. What's your favorite YouTube channel?   [I like...]

3. Do you like Two OK Rock? I always watch them on YouTube.   [Really? I...]

Communication Strategy

Show your interest

Show your interest in what somebody is talking about. If you do, they will probably talk more. Use these phrases below. Show your interest to your partner.

Wow! / Really? / Thank you. / That's very nice of you to say so. / Is that right?

Your partner says:
1. I paid 15,000 yen for my new haircut.
2. I have a friend who makes over 500,000 yen a month on YouTube.
3. I like your voice. It's so deep.
4. I saw our English teacher on the train this morning.
5. Did you know "umami" and "panko" are words in English now too?

Active Listening

 DL 40   CD1-40

Listen to the conversation between the two speakers. Find the answers to the questions below with your partner.

1. Where are Seira and Noah from?

2. What's the weather like today?

3. What did Kenta and Yuka do?

4. What's the name of the song they're talking about?

5. Where are they talking?

Read the passages below. What social networking service is each passage about?

To make money on ¹ (   ), you must have a minimum of 1,000 subscribers. Then you can get a 45% cut of ad revenue. Generally speaking, you make between $3 and $5 for

5 the same number of views on your videos. You can make a lot of money if you can create interesting videos.

² (   ), owned by a Chinese company, is a video-sharing app that allows users to share 15-second videos

10 on any topic, such as dance videos, magic tricks, and comedy videos. Due to the short format, the video creation takes much less time. It's very popular among teenagers.

³ (   ) is an American social networking service on which users post and interact with messages less than 280 characters. Users can post

15 and retweet tweets. Former American President Trump used this social media service very often, but he was banned from using it.

⁴ (   ) is an American photo sharing social networking service. Posts can be shared publicly or with pre-approved followers. The service also has messaging features and a "stories" feature with each post accessible for only

20 24 hours.

A Fill in the blanks with either TikTok, YouTube, Twitter, or Instagram.

Quick Search on the Web 🔍

What are the top three social networking services in the world? How about in the U.S. and in Japan? Use key words such as "SNS users in …" or "most used SNS in…" Fill in the chart.

	World	U.S.	Japan
No. 1			
No. 2			
No. 3			

Activator
Open-ended Practice

A Look at your partner. Imagine you happen to be in the same elevator, and you do not want to be quiet. Follow the directions and start small talk with them You have to keep talking (about anything you like) for about two minutes. Find a new partner and do it again.

Directions

1. Greet them.   [*A:* Hi, how are you doing? *B:* Hi,....]

2. Talk about the weather.   [*A:* Nice/Rainy/Hot/ ..., isn't it? *B:* Exactly....]

3. Talk about some news or sporting event you saw recently.
                                                  [*A:* Did you see...? *B:* Yeah....]

4. Say nice things about something they are wearing.   [*A:* I like your.... *B:* I go it at....]

5. Say something nice about their hairstyle or makeup.   [*A:* Nice.... *B:* Thank you....]

6. Talk about any interesting videos or pictures you saw on social media.
                                                  [*A:* I saw.... *B:* Really?....]

7. Ask which floor they want to go to.   [*A:* Which floor...? *B:* XX, please.]

8. Stop the conversation by saying, "It was nice talking to you."
                                                  [*A:* It was...., *B:* Yes, it was....]

B Do you agree or disagree with the statement below? In a group of three or four, discuss your opinions.

"We shouldn't sit quietly if there is someone sitting right next to us on the Shinkansen or an airplane."

Cultures / Idols / Anime

Focus

Asking and
Answering
Questions

⚡ Brainstorm

A Pair up and talk about yourself and your partner. Examples are shown in [ ].

1. *A:* Do you have a favorite anime?

B: Yes, my favorite one is _____.

[*One Piece* / *Princess Mononoke* / *My Neighbor Totoro*]

2. *A:* Do you think Japanese idols can sing well?

B: I think they _____ because _____.

[can / can't]   [some are not singers / they take lessons]

3. *A:* Why do some Japanese students go to the restroom together?

B: I think they _____.   [just like to / are more comfortable that way]

4. *A:* What is your blood type?

B: It's _____. Why do you ask?

[A / O / B / AB]

B Switch roles. This time add one or two extra comments. See the example below. Go over 1-4 above again. Below is an example for exercise number one.

A: Do you have a favorite anime?

B: Yes, my favorite one is *My Neighbor Totoro.*

A: Really? I like that anime too. Who is your favorite character?

B: I like Mei. She is so innocent. Who is yours?

A: I like Nekobasu - The Cat Bus.

 **Dialogue** DL 42 CD2-01

Olga asks her friend Masato about *otaku*. Role-play the dialogue with your partner. Then switch roles and practice again.

Olga: Can I ask you a question, Masato?

Masato: Sure, Olga. What is it?

Olga: What are "otaku?"

Masato: Where did you hear that word?

Olga: Well, Mari called me an otaku, but I don't know what it is.

Masato: Uh-huh... An otaku is like a nerd.

Olga: Oh, that's why she called me an otaku.

Masato: What do you mean? Are you crazy about something?

Olga: Yes, about Japanese anime. I just love *Naruto*.

Masato: Really? Me, too.

A Ask at least two questions about the dialogue to your partner. Take turns.

B Replace the underlined parts with your own information and practice the conversation again. Be original and creative. Try to add a few more lines at the end.

C Listen to the rest of the conversation and ask the questions to each other.

 DL 43 CD2-02

1. What did Masato learn from watching *Naruto*?

2. How many years has Masato been watching *Naruto*?

3. How many episodes are there in the whole series?

4. What is the reason why Olga became interested in Japan?

5. What are they doing this summer?

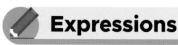 # Expressions

A Practice each dialogue with your partner.

1. **A:** You got a minute? **I have a question**.
   B: <u>Sure</u>. What is it?

2. **A:** **What does** "<u>Yoroshiku</u>" **mean**?
   B: That's a tough question. It means <u>a lot</u>.

3. **A:** **Is it true that** <u>traditionally only women give chocolate on Valentine's Day in Japan</u>?
   B: Yes, and <u>men give a return gift a month later on White Day</u>.

4. **A:** **Why** do Japanese people mention blood types so often?
   B: Some people believe blood type <u>can tell a lot about personality</u>.

5. **A:** Why do some Americans wear <u>only a T-shirt</u> in winter?
   B: **Is that strange for you?**

B Replace the underlined words with your own words and practice again. Be original and creative.

 # Interactive Practice

A Find the corresponding response with your partner. Draw lines while you're talking.

1. **A:** What does "hekomu" mean?   ·

2. **A:** Can I ask you a question?   ·

3. **A:** Why can't some Japanese idols sing well?   ·

4. **A:** How do you say "noto pasokon" · in English?

5. **A:** Why do you make a noise when you eat noodles?   ·

· **B:** It's called a laptop.

· **B:** Because they are not singers.

· **B:** Sure, but make it short, please.

· **B:** Well, it means you're depressed.

· **B:** Believe me. It actually tastes better.

Quick Search on the Web 🔍

Find out what the most popular Japanese anime in the world is. How about the bestselling manga in the world? (key words: most popular anime, bestselling manga)

Anime: Manga:

B Role-play the dialogue with your partner twice. First, choose the appropriate response from the list below. Next, complete the dialogue again using your own information.

> *that's a tough question   someone's personality   AB*
> *cool and organized   I hope it's not a difficult one*

A: Can I ask you a question?

B: _____.

A: Why do Japanese people mention blood type so often?

B: _____. Does that seem strange to you?

A: Yeah, I didn't know my blood type until I came to Japan.

B: Really? Many Japanese people believe blood type can tell a lot about

_____.

A: Is that right?

B: What's your blood type?

A: _____.

B: Then you are _____.

A: Really? I'm glad to hear that.

C You are an international student who just arrived in Japan. Ask the following questions about the topic below. Add one extra question to ask your partner. Follow the example.

> **Example**

wear kimonos more often [Why...]

A: Why don't Japanese people wear kimonos more often?

B: Well, it's because they are very expensive and not practical.

A: How about you? Do you sometimes wear a kimono?

B: Yes, but only at summer festivals.

1. some college students study much [Why don't...]
2. Pachinko parlors [What are...]
3. many adults read comics [Why do...]
4. the most popular idol group [Who is...]
5. so few garbage cans [Why are there...]
6. people bow while talking on the phone [Why do...]
7. trains come exactly on time [Why do...]
8. drunk people everywhere at night [Why are there...]

Ask many questions

Questions are an expression of your interest in the person you're talking to. It's actually more polite to ask questions than not to ask questions. Take turns asking as many questions as possible to your partner in two minutes.

Example

A: Where do you live, Juri?

B: I'm from Chiba. How about you, Taiga?

A: I'm from Osaka.

B: Where in Osaka are you from?

A: An area near USJ.

B: Really? I love USJ.

A: I don't anymore. I've been there too many times.

B: Oh, I love it there. Do you want to...?
How about Disneyland? Do you like Disneyland?

Active Listening   DL 45   CD2-04

What are they talking about? Choose the right topic from the list below.

Tea Ceremony	*Miso*	*Pachinko*
New Year's Eve Bells	*Noisy Japanese people*	

1. _____

2. _____

3. _____

4. _____

5. _____

Active Reading

DL 46   CD2-05

Scan through the passages about things unique to Japan and do exercise A below.

1. Japanese robotic smart (   )
are both cool and crazy. They talk and
play sounds when being used so that the
peeing sound isn't heard by other people.

5 A bidet and dryer are attached, too. You
won't even need to use your (   )
or paper anymore in Japan.

2. In Tokyo, people stand on the left side while
keeping the right side of (   )

10 for rushing pedestrians. This is the other way around in Osaka. So be careful
when riding (   ) in Japan, you might be blocking someone's way!

3. If you are a big anime or video game fan, then Akihabara is your (   ).
Akihabara used to just be a home for electronic gadgets, but now it is also
known as the anime capital of Japan. You can see cute girls dressed up in maid

15 costumes, (   ) walking by, and anime-themed cafes... anything you can imagine.

A Read the passages about some aspects of Japanese culture below. Fill in the blanks
with appropriate words listed below. Some words may be used twice or not at all. Be
careful!

| *escalators* | *cosplayers* | *paradise* | *toilets* | *hands* | *open* |

Quick Search on the Web 🔍

Search for things international visitors find strange about Japan. List at least two and share them
in class. (Key words: weird, strange things, Japan)

1. _____

2. _____

Activator
Open-ended Practice

A Look at the pictures below. Imagine you're not familiar with Japanese culture. Ask at least three questions about each picture. Sample questions are listed below.

octopus dumplings

a large mortar/usu

sports day

Sample Questions:

1. What is this?
2. What do you call this in Japanese?
3. What does it taste like?
4. How do you make it?
5. How do you use it?
6. Do you have one?
7. Where and when can I see one?
8. Are they expensive?
9. Is it fun?
10. What is it for?
11. Do you like them?
12. (your original question)

B Imagine you are a tourism promotion specialist from the Japanese government sent overseas. Make a short presentation to your partner on why people in the world should visit Japan. Give at least three reasons. Your partner needs to ask you some questions. Some possible reasons are:

1. temples and shrines are incredible
2. the cleanest country in the world
3. million-dollar views of cherry blossoms and autumn leaves
4. food is great
5. very safe for solo travel
6. people are generally really kind
7. center of Japanese anime and manga

Unit 10 Music

Focus

Asking for Permission / Making Suggestions

 Brainstorm

A Pair up and talk about yourself and your partner. Examples are shown in [ ].

1. *A:* Who is your favorite singer or band?

B: My favorite singer/band is _____. [Ed Sheeran / Mr. Children]

2. *A:* What kind of music do you like?

B: I like _____. [rock / K-pop / rap]

3. *A:* What do you think of (the name of your favorite band)?

B: Oh, I _____ because their music is _____.

[like / don't like] [great / too aggressive]

4. *A:* Do you go to concerts?

B: Yes, _____. [I love music festivals / I never miss a _____ concert]

No, _____. [I hate crowded places / I rarely go to concerts]

B Switch roles. This time add one or two extra comments. See the example below. Go over 1-4 above again. Below is an example for exercise number one.

A: Who is your favorite singer or band?

B: My favorite band is The Beatles.

A: You like old music?

B: No, not usually. The Beatles are old, but their music is timeless. You should listen to them. They have great songs that people in every generation love.

 # Dialogue

Joshua and Rinka are in the car and listening to music on the radio. Role-play the dialogue with your partner. Then switch roles and practice again.

Joshua: Can I turn the volume up?

Rinka: Sure. Do you like this music?

Joshua: Yeah, I love <u>the Activators</u>.

Rinka: Me, too. I love the <u>rhythm</u> of their music.

Joshua: Their lyrics are very <u>powerful</u>, too.

Rinka: I agree. Hey, did you know they're coming to <u>Tokyo this fall</u>?

Joshua: Really? I'd love to go to their concert.

Rinka: Do you think we can get tickets?

Joshua: Well, if we try together, we may get lucky.

Rinka: What do you mean?

A Ask at least two questions about the dialogue to your partner. Take turns.

B Replace the underlined parts with your own information and practice the conversation again. Be original and creative. Try to add a few more lines at the end.

C Listen to the rest of the conversation. Circle either True, False, or Not sure.

1. Rinka and Joshua are trying to get two tickets each.   True / False / Not sure
2. If they get four tickets, they will probably cancel two of them.   True / False / Not sure
3. Rinka usually has to be home by 10:00 at night.   True / False / Not sure
4. Rinka is probably going to ask her parents to join them for the concert.   True / False / Not sure
5. Rinka's parents are big fans of the Activators.   True / False / Not sure

✏️ **Expressions**

🎧 DL 49   💿 CD2-08

A Practice each dialogue with your partner.

1. *A:* **Can I** borrow your <u>music player</u>?
   B: **Sure.** But please give it back soon.

2. *A:* **Is it OK if** I <u>copy this CD</u>?
   B: **I'd rather you didn't.**

3. *A:* **Do you mind if** I use your <u>ear buds</u>?
   B: No, I don't mind. Go ahead.

4. *A:* What should I do with these old records?
   B: **Why don't you** sell them <u>online</u>?

5. *A:* Do you think I should try to go pro?
   B: **Sure, why not?** I think you're <u>very talented</u>.

B Replace the underlined words with your own words and practice again. Be original and creative.

🎵 **Interactive Practice**

A Ask what types of music your partner likes. Number them from 1 (most favorite) through 10 (least favorite).

> **Example**

What kind music do you like best? How about the second best?

J-pop (   ) jazz (   ) K-pop (   ) rock (   )

metal (   ) hip-hop (   ) reggae (   ) classical (   )

country (   ) folk (   )

Quick Search on the Web 🔍

Choose one kind of music and search for information about how it started. Share it with your classmates. (Key words: origin, history, hip-hop/metal/rap/jazz/K-pop)

When: Where:

Who: Others:

B Ask your partner if you can do the following things. Your partner needs to respond. Take turns. Use the following expressions.

> *A: Can I...? / Is it OK if I...? / Do you mind if I...? / May I...?*
>
> *B: Sure / Go ahead. / No problem / I'd rather you didn't. / Sorry, you can't because....*

1. borrow your guitar for a month?
2. come to your house this Saturday evening?
3. ask your sister out to a concert on Friday night?
4. sing this song together with you?
5. (your own request) _____

C You're in the following situations. Ask your partner for advice. Your partner needs to respond. Take turns. Use the following expressions.

> *A: I want to.... / I'm thinking about.... / Any good advice for me? / What do you think? / What should I do?*
>
> *B: You should.... / If I were you, I would.... / Why don't you...? / I suggest that you....*

1. You hate karaoke, but your partner loves it.

Example

A: I hate karaoke, but Jun always wants to go to karaoke when we go on a date. What should I do?

B: Why don't you just tell him that?

A: I have many times.

B: Well, if I were you, I would tell him to date someone else then if he wants to go to karaoke on every date.

2. You want to learn how to play the drums, but you can't find a teacher.
3. You want to be a professional rock singer, but your parents are against it.
4. You love to sing, but you're a horrible singer.
5. (Your own concern) _____

Communication Strategy

Yes/No first, reasons later

Say "No" or "Yes" first if someone asks a favor of you, then give your reason. Do not give reasons first because that may confuse the person you're talking to. Number 1 is done for you as an example. Say "Yes, I'd love to;" "No, I'd rather not;" or say "I don't think I can" first, then give some reasons. Practice with your partner.

1. **A:** We need a bassist. Would you like to join our band?
   B: Yes, I'd love to. I've always wanted to join a band.
2. **A:** Can I borrow some money? I'm broke, but I really want to go to this concert.
   B: _____.
3. **A:** Do you mind if I smoke here?
   B: _____.
4. **A:** Please let me copy your notes for this class.
   B: _____.

🎧 Active Listening

 DL 50   CD2-09

Listen to the two conversations. What are they talking about? What is the advice given? Take notes and share them with your partner.

Conversation 1

Conversation 2

Read the passages about musicians or genres of music and do exercise A below.

1. This American music genre was made from a mixture of various songs and styles from New England to New Orleans. It included hymns, folk songs, spirituals, work songs, gospel, and blues. In the South, the rhythm of African drums was woven into it creating a new genre of American music called (   ).

2. Inherently hybrid in origin, this genre of music includes elements of African American blues music and white country and western music. Emerging around 1954-55, this style of music was initially called "(   ) 'n' roll." Queen, the Rolling Stones, and King Gnu are among the famous groups in this genre.

3. When (   ) debuted, they wore the same suits and had the same hair style, mop haircuts. They had 20 number one singles in the U.S. and 17 in Britain. They were critically acclaimed, and some say they were the greatest composers since Beethoven. One of their members was shot dead in front of his apartment in New York in 1980.

A Which musician or what kind of music are they talking about? Write down the names of the famous bands or genres of music.

Quick Search on the Web 🔍

Find out as much information as possible about The Beatles, such as who they are, where they were born, how many songs they wrote, how many years the band existed, which members are still alive, why some consider them to be the greatest composers since Beethoven, etc. Share it in class.

_____

_____

Activator
Open-ended Practice

A Stand up and move around the classroom. You will have 5 minutes. Find someone who has done the following things. If the person says, "Yes," ask their name. Ask as many different people as possible. Number 1 is done for you.

Someone who: **List of Names**

1. **can play the guitar or the piano**
   A: Can you play the guitar or the piano?
   B: Yes, I can play the guitar.
   A: Good. May I have your name?   (   )

2. often goes to concerts   (   )
3. can sing a rap song   (   )
4. likes K-pop   (   )
5. loves to go to karaoke   (   )
6. thinks Justin Bieber is a great singer   (   )
7. can sing "Yesterday" or "Let it be"   (   )
8. has been in a rock band   (   )
9. has more than 100 songs on their phone (   )
10. would like to learn to play a musical instrument someday
                                               (   )

B Discuss your favorite songs with a partner or in a group. Ask the following questions and some more of your own. Take turns.

1. What is your favorite song?
   Why do you like it?
   When do you listen to it?
   Do you have any stories you'd like to tell me about that song or the artist?
   Tell me more about that song.

2. Do you know any other good songs that you'd recommend listening to?
   Who sings it?
   What is it about?
   Why is it so good?
   Can you sing it a bit?

Unit 11 Relationships

Focus

Describing People / Expressing Likes and Dislikes

 Brainstorm

A Pair up and talk about yourself and your partner. Examples are shown in [ ].

1. *A:* What would your ideal partner be like?
   B: Well, they should be _____, _____ and
   very _____. [smart / honest / funny / generous]

2. *A:* Can you tell me more about their personality?
   B: Well, they would be _____, _____ and
   very _____. [friendly / talkative / easy-going / outgoing]

3. *A:* What qualities do you look for in a future partner?
   B: I look for _____ and _____.
   [love / sense of humor / openness / looks]

4. *A:* Would you like (somebody famous) as your future partner?
   B: That would be _____ because he/she is _____.
   [ideal / OK / terrible]   [good-looking / warm-hearted / intelligent]

B Switch roles. This time add one or two extra comments. See the example below. Go over 1-4 above again. Below is an example for exercise number one.

A: What would your ideal partner(s) be like?
B: Well, they should be smart, honest, and rich.
A: That's a lot to ask.
B: I also look for a good sense of humor. How about you?
A: Well, I want my partner to be....

Dialogue

Jessica has a new boyfriend. She is describing him to Taiga. Role-play the dialogue with your partner. Then switch roles and practice again.

Taiga: I heard you've got a new boyfriend.

Jessica: Yeah, his name is Nori. He is smart, sincere, and funny.

Taiga: He sounds great.

Jessica: He speaks English really well, too.

Taiga: Wow, that's perfect.

Jessica: Not quite. He has no sense of fashion.

Taiga: There's nothing wrong with that.

Jessica: Well...

Taiga: Wait, does Nori wear black all the time?

Jessica: How did you know that?

Taiga: I think I know who he is.

A Ask at least two questions about the dialogue to your partner. Take turns.

B Replace the underlined parts with your own information and practice the conversation again. Change "he" and "his" accordingly. Be original and creative. Try to add a few more lines at the end.

C Listen to the rest of the conversation. Circle either True, False, or Not sure.

1. Taiga and Nori are in the aikido club.	True / False / Not sure
2. Nori is older than Taiga.	True / False / Not sure
3. Taiga is very good at aikido.	True / False / Not sure
4. Some international students are in the aikido club.	True / False / Not sure
5. Jessica will try practicing aikido today.	True / False / Not sure

Expressions

A Practice each dialogue with your partner.

1. **A: Do you mind talking about** your <u>brother</u>?
   B: Not at all. <u>He</u> is <u>talkative</u>, <u>sociable</u>, and very <u>independent</u>.

2. **A: What is** your <u>girlfriend</u> **like**?
   B: Well, <u>she</u> is <u>sincere</u>, but a bit <u>shy</u>.

3. **A: Can you describe** your <u>pet</u>?
   B: Well, <u>Junior</u> is very <u>cute</u> and <u>playful</u>.

4. **A: How do you like** my new <u>sneakers</u>?
   B: I like <u>them</u> a lot. <u>They're</u> really <u>cool</u>.

5. **A: What do you think of** <u>Kenji</u>?
   B: I <u>like him a lot... as a friend</u>.

B Replace the underlined words with your own words and practice again. Be original and creative.

 # Interactive Practice

A Circle the words that describe the appearance and personality of someone you know. Circle one or two in each category. Tell your partner more about the person.

Appearance:

average build, has a buzz cut, wears glasses, carries a red backpack, dresses nicely

Personality:

Positive — reliable, generous, punctual, honest, considerate, organized
Negative — unreliable, rude, boring, lazy, forgetful, short-tempered
Neutral — easygoing, outgoing, quiet, talkative, serious, sociable

---

Quick Search on the Web 🔍

Find some words with similar and opposite meanings to the following words. (Key words: thesaurus, synonyms, antonyms)

	Similar meaning	Opposite meaning
friendly	( )	( )
honest	( )	( )
well-dressed	( )	( )

B Describe someone in your classroom. But you cannot talk about his or her physical features such as being tall or having big eyes. Your partner needs to guess who the person is. Take turns. Use the example below.

Example

Partner: Tell me about someone in this class. What is that person like?

You: Yes, he/she is _____ and _____.

Partner: Does he/she wear glasses?

You: Yes.

Partner: OK. What is he/she wearing?

You: He/She is wearing _____.

Partner: What is his/her personality like? Is he/she _____?

You: No, he/she is rather _____ and a bit _____.

Partner: I think you're talking about our teacher.

You: Bingo!!

C Describe one of your favorite cartoon characters. Your partner needs to draw a picture of the character. See if the drawing looks like the character. Then tell your partner why you like the character. Take turns. Follow the example.

Example

A: Can you tell me about your favorite cartoon character?

B: Sure. He's an imaginary mouse-like animal.

A: What color is he?

B: I will not tell you. If I do, you can guess too easily.

A: OK. Does he have a kind of triangular tail?

B: Yes. His face is kind of round.

A: And his cheeks have red spots?

B: Yes, and he has long ears.

A: Does he have electrical abilities?

B: Yes, he does.

A: I know who he is. He's Pikachu, isn't he?

B: Yes. I love Pikachu.

A: Me, too. Why do you like him so much?

B: Well, he's not only cute but he also cares about other Pokémon.

What would you say ...in...?

If you can't think of the words you want to say, don't be quiet. Ask somebody around you. Practice with your partner. Here is an example.

A: How would you say "kanji ii hito" in English?
B: I think it's "a friendly person."
A: Oh, that's easy. Thank you.

1. someone you can trust   (reliable or trustworthy)
2. *bozu atama* in English   (shaved head or buzz cut)
3. someone you loved for the first time   (first crush or first love)
4. *suki desu* in Korean   (saranghaeyo)

Active Listening

DL 55   CD2-14

Listen to the talk between two freshmen on campus. They're talking about seniors—senpai in the dance club. Find out who they are talking about. Write down their names in the boxes next to the person in the picture.

Active Reading DL 56 CD2-15

Below are four different answers to the question: "What is your ideal partner like?". Read them aloud to your partner. To what extent do you agree? Number them from 1 (strongly agree) to 4 (do not agree at all) accordingly.

Joung-Hee: I don't want to marry someone boring. I need someone who can have an intelligent conversation with me and who can also make me laugh every day. I need somebody
5 with a great sense of humor and great intelligence. (   )

Miki: My ideal future partner has to be rich and let me travel overseas at least once a year. He should also have knowledge about savings and investments. If you have
10 money, you tend to be more relaxed and generous. (   )

Rob: I need somebody who is kind, loving, and slow to anger. Basically, I want somebody to genuinely love me and accept me as I am. We should try to make our relationship better with lots of care and affection for each other. (   )

Adam: I would need someone that understands my need for alone time. I am intro-
15 verted and can get exhausted being around people all day. Sometimes I just need to go to a dark room and sit there by myself for an hour. (   )

A Discuss which qualities for an ideal partner are most important to you?

Example

A: Of course love is the most important but I'd like to marry someone rich.
B: To me, it's intelligence and a good sense of humor.
A: Oh, why?

1. Love and care for each other.

2. Money and career

3. No arrest record

4. Trust, respect, honesty, and kindness

5. Emotionally stable

6. Spending time with each other

7. Intelligence

8. Sense of humor

9. Sharing similar interests and values

10. (your choice) _____

Quick Search on the Web

Find out what qualities people want in a good spouse in the U.S.? Do you see any differences between Japan and the U.S.? (key words: qualities of a good spouse, ideal husband/wife in the U.S.)

Activator
Open-ended Practice

A Pair up and talk about either someone famous you like or yourself. Find out what your partner likes or dislikes about their/your fashion, hair style, possessions (pencil cases, bags, computers) or anything else they have. Take turns. Find another partner and do it again. Follow the examples.

Example

1. **fashion**

   A: I love Lady Gaga. How do you like her fashion sense? I think she's very fashionable.

   B: Yes, she is, but I don't like her fashion sense. It's too loud and extreme.

   A: That's the point. She is not afraid to wear anything she likes.

   B: Maybe so, but I just don't like it.

   A: How about you? Who do you like?

   B: I like EOM. I think their stylist has very good fashion sense.

   A: I agree. But something I don't like about them is...

2. **hair style**

   A: How do you like my hairstyle?

   B: It looks very good on you. You just got your hair cut?

   A: Yes, at Activator Hair Design in Ginza.

   B: How about mine?

   A: It's OK, but you may want to do something with your bangs?

   B: Is there something wrong?

   A: I think they're a bit too long.

3. **possessions**   [pencil cases / bags / computers]

4. **your own choice**   [sense of humor / personalities / social activities]

B Do you agree or disagree with the following statements? Discuss them below in groups of three or four.

1. You should only marry or date someone whose room is tidy and clean.
2. If a couple doesn't feel excited any more when they spend time together, they should break up right away.

Unit 12 Traveling Overseas

Focus

Survival English

 Brainstorm

A Pair up and talk about yourself and your partner. Examples are shown in [   ].

1. *A:* Where in the world would you like to travel? Why?
   B: I'd like to go to _____ because _____.
   [Italy / Cambodia]   [I like ancient buildings / I'd like to see Angkor Wat]

2. *A:* Would you like to study abroad? Why or why not?
   B: Yes, I'd like to study in _____   [Australia / France]
   because I'd like to _____. [improve my English skills / study fashion]
   No, I wouldn't because _____.   [I'm not interested / I'm scared]

3. *A:* Do you prefer to travel by train, car, or airplane?
   B: I prefer to travel by _____.   [train / car / airplane]

4. *A:* What is the best place you've ever visited? Why was it the best?
   B: It was _____. It was the best because _____.
   [Nikko / Hokkaido]   [the nature was amazing / people were very kind]

B Switch roles. This time add one or two extra comments. See the example below. Go over 1-4 above again. Below is an example for exercise number one.

   A: Where in the world would you like to travel? Why?
   B: I'd like to go to Italy because I like ancient buildings.
   A: Like the Colosseum?
   B: Yes, and the Leaning Tower of Pisa.
   A: Hey, can I go with you? I'd like to see them, too.
   B: Why not? That'd be wonderful.

Hina and two of her friends just arrived at Kennedy International Airport in New York. They want to go to downtown New York. Hina is talking to a man at the information desk. Role-play the dialogue with your partner. Then switch roles and practice again.

Hina: Hi, we'd like to go to down-town <u>New York</u>. What are our options?

Man: I suggest you take a <u>shuttle bus</u> or a <u>taxi</u>.

Hina: There isn't a train?

Man: There is, but you have so much luggage. I wouldn't suggest taking the train.

Hina: OK. How much is the fare if we take <u>a taxi</u>?

Man: About <u>70 dollars</u> including tip.

Hina: That's <u>not bad</u>. Can you tell me where the <u>taxi stand</u> is?

Man: It's right outside. Go out the doors and turn <u>right</u>. It's just past <u>Enterprise</u>.

Hina: Thank you.

Man: No problem.

A Ask at least two questions about the dialogue to your partner. Take turns.

B Replace the underlined parts with your own information and practice the conversation again. Be original and creative. Try to add a few more lines at the end.

C Listen to the rest of the conversation and answer the questions.

 DL 58   CD2-17

1. What is Enterprise?
2. How many people are traveling together including Hina?
3. How much is the insurance for a car for three days?
4. According to the man, what is very expensive in Manhattan?
5. How are they going to get downtown?

 **Expressions**   DL 59   CD2-18

A Practice each dialogue with your partner.

1. *A:* **Could you tell me** where I can catch <u>a bus</u>?
   B: Down that way. You'll see the sign.
2. *A:* **I have a reservation.** My name is <u>Marino Kawata</u>.
   B: Yes, <u>Ms. Kawata</u>. We have <u>two twin</u> rooms for you.
3. *A:* **I'd like to check in, please**.
   B: May I have your <u>last name</u>?
4. *A:* **I'll have** the <u>seafood combo</u>.
   B: OK. Anything to drink?
5. *A:* Here's <u>20 dollars</u>. **Keep the change.**
   B: Thank you, <u>sir</u>. **Have a good day.**

B Replace the underlined words with your own words and practice again. Be original and creative.

 Interactive Practice

A Pair up and find an appropriate response. Practice aloud with your partner. There may be more than one correct answer.

A:

1. What's the purpose of your trip?
2. It's 15 pounds.
3. What's the cheapest way to downtown LA?
4. Could you give me a wake-up call?
5. What's a good restaurant to try around here?

B:

· *I don't know. I'm a tourist here.*
· *Sure. What time?*
· *Taking a bus.*
· *Sightseeing.*
· *Here's 20. Keep the change.*

Quick Search on the Web 🔍

Find out some options for getting to downtown London from Heathrow Airport. Which way is the fastest? Which is the cheapest? Which would you take? How about from where you live to the nearest international airport?

	Heathrow Airport		Your closest airport	
fastest	(	)	(	)
cheapest	(	)	(	)
your choice	(	)	(	)

B You're working as a server at a Japanese restaurant in an international airport near your city. Help the customer. Pair up and act out the conversation. Switch roles and do it again.

A: Are you ready to order?

B: I can't decide. Do you have any recommendations?

A: Well, I like the katsudon and the _____.

B: OK, I'll try the _____, then.

A: Great. Anything to drink?

B: Yes. I'll have _____.

A: Thank you. I'll be right back with your _____ and _____.

B: Wait. Can I ask you a question?

A: Of course.

B: What's the best way to go to _____?

A: I suggest you take _____. It's slow, but it's the cheapest.

B: I'm in a hurry.

A: Then you should take _____.

B: How much would the fare be?

A: I think it's around _____ yen.

B: Thank you.

C Act out the situation below with your partner. Read your part only. When you're done, do it again. This time do <u>not</u> look at the sample conversation.

A's situation: You're at the reception desk of a hotel. You don't have a reservation, but you want a room for tonight. You're very tired, and you don't want to spend much money for the room. Negotiate the price.

B's situation: You're a hotel clerk at the reception desk. You only have one twin room left. The room charge is 200 dollars per night plus tax, but since it's the last room left, you don't mind giving it for 100-150 dollars.

Example

A: Hello. I don't have a reservation, but do you have a room for tonight?

B: Yes, but we have only one _____ left. It's _____ dollars per night.

A: That's kind of expensive. Can you give me a discount?

B: Well, I can give it to you for _____ dollars since it's the last room left.

A: I'm a poor student. How about _____ dollars?

B: OK. I'll make an exception and give you a very special discount price.

A: Thank you so much. You're a life saver.

B: You're welcome. Now, may I have your name?

A: Yes, my name is _____.

Communication **Strategy**

Check your own understanding

If you're not sure you understand someone, check your understanding by saying
phrases like *You mean... or Are you saying...?*

Example

A: Sorry, the check-in time is 3:00.
B: Are you saying we can't check-in until 3:00?

Check your understanding using the phrases above. Practice with your partner.
1. Sorry, there are no trains here. [I have to take a taxi or a bus?]
2. I can't find your name on our reservation list. [I can't stay here tonight?]
3. You don't have to order kimchi in the restaurant. [it comes with the meals for free?]

 Active Listening DL 60 CD2-19

Listen to the recorded conversations of people who are traveling overseas. Where are they?
Choose the best answer from the list.

1. _____

2. _____

3. _____

Airport

Grocery store

Post office

Japanese restaurant

On a street

Read the descriptions of some famous places in the world.

1. (   ) is a must-see
   for many visitors. Visitors love the
   amazing food, friendly people,
   affordable prices, and the scary
5 rides and brilliant Harry Potter
   World at Universal Studios Japan.
   You could also visit here as a day
   trip from Kyoto.

2. (   ) is a holy
10 city for three major religions: Christianity, Judaism, and Islam. It is located in
   Israel. There are many historical sites that you can visit. The Dead Sea is also
   located close to this city.

3. If you like the outdoors, then you will love (   ) located in
   Wyoming in the U.S. Some great things to see here are geysers (hot springs
15 that shoot hot water high into the air), animals such as bison, bears, and
   moose, and hot springs that come in many different colors.

4. (   ) is an ancient city in Peru. It is 80 kilometers north-
   west of Cuzco. The Incas built this city around 1,450 A.D. but abandoned it a
   century later at the time of the Spanish conquest.

A Work with your partner to fill in the blanks with the appropriate name of the places.

Machu Picchu   *Alaska*   *Rome*   *Grand Canyon National Park*
Yellowstone National Park   *Jerusalem*   *Nara*   *Osaka*

Quick Search on the Web

Pair up and choose a place in the world from the list below. Find out where it is and what it is famous for. Share pictures with each other.

Grand Canyon National Park   Cappadocia   Cotswolds

Activator
Open-ended Practice

A You're planning an international trip with your partner for your next vacation. Ask your partner the following questions and decide where you want to go and what you want to do.

1. What country should we visit?
2. What cities or places in that country should we visit?
3. What should we see or do there?
4. Are there any other places in the country we should visit?
5. What gifts from Japan shall we bring in case we make friends there?
6. How much money should we take?
7. Should we work part-time together to make money before we go?
8. If yes, do you know any good places that we can work at?
9. How many days do we need for this trip?
10. Are we staying in one country or visiting other neighboring countries too?
11. Do you want to ask other people to come along? If so, who?
12. How will we get around when we are there?
13. Should we rent a car? Do you have a driver's license?
14. (Your own choice) _____?

B How would you answer the following questions? Discuss in a small group or in class.

Topic 1: Is it better to book a hotel in advance or walk in?

You don't have to worry about where to stay if you have hotel reservations for the entire trip. However, if you don't, you're free to stay at any place for a longer or shorter period of time than planned. Your trip will be more flexible. Which do you prefer, booking a hotel in advance or walking in? Why?

Topic 2: Is it better to move around or to stay in one place?

If you stay in one place for a long time, you can take your time to enjoy reading books or shopping. If you move around, you can visit many famous sightseeing spots, but you may get tired. Which do you prefer, moving around or staying in one place? Why?

Shopping

Focus

Expressions for Negotiation and Shopping

⚡ Brainstorm

A Pair up and talk about yourself and your partner. Examples are shown in [   ].

1. **A:** Do you like to go shopping?
   B: I _____ to go shopping because _____.
   [like / don't like]   [I can/cannot buy what I want / It makes me feel happy/tired]

2. **A:** Where do usually go shopping?
   B: I usually _____.   [shop online / go to Takashimaya]

3. **A:** Do you ask for a discount when you buy expensive goods?
   B: Yes / No, because _____.
   [I'm buying expensive stuff / I'm too shy / It depends]

4. **A:** Do you like to buy big name brand goods?
   B: I _____ buying big name brand goods because they are _____.
   [like / don't like]   [well-made / well-designed / overpriced / too showy]

B Switch roles. This time add one or two extra comments. See the example below. Go over 1-4 above again. Below is an example for exercise number one.

   A: Do you like to go shopping?
   B: I don't like to go shopping because I get tired easily.
   A: <u>Then how do you get the things you want?</u>
   B: <u>I shop online on Amazon or Rakuten. It's easier and faster.</u>

Dialogue

🎧 DL 62   ◎ CD2-21

Keita is trying to buy some T-shirts at a flea market for tourists in Hawaii. Role-play the dialogue with your partner. Then switch roles and practice again.

Keita: Do you have the same <u>T-shirt</u> in <u>white</u>?

Vender: Sorry, these come in <u>red</u> and <u>blue</u> only.

Keita: Then, do you have this red shirt in a <u>smaller</u> size?

Vender: Is a <u>medium</u> small enough for you?

Keita: No, I need a <u>small</u>. They're souvenirs for my <u>twin little sisters</u>.

Vender: Okay, we have the red in <u>a small</u>.

Keita: Good. I'll take <u>two small red T-shirts then</u>.

Vender: Thank you. That'll be <u>24</u> dollars plus tax.

Keita: Can you give me a discount? I'm getting <u>two</u>.

Vender: Sorry. We can't.

A Ask at least two questions about the dialogue to your partner. Take turns.

B Replace the underlined parts with your own information and practice the conversation again. Be original and creative. Try to add a few more lines at the end.

C Listen to the rest of the conversation and answer the questions.

🎧 DL 63   ◎ CD2-22

1. Did Keita get a discount?

2. How many T-shirts did Keita get?

3. How much is Keita going to pay?

4. How many blue shirts did Keita get all together?

5. How is Keita going to pay?

 **Expressions**

A Practice each dialogue with your partner.

1. **A:** Anything I can help you with?
   B: Thank you, but **I'm just looking around**.

2. **A:** Do you have this in <u>a smaller size</u>?
   B: Yes, we do. What size are you looking for?

3. **A:** **I'm looking for** <u>the sweatshirts</u>.
   B: They are right over here.

4. **A:** It looks <u>really nice</u> on you.
   B: Thank you. **I'll take it**.

5. **A:** That'll be <u>$24.50</u>.
   B: **Do you take credit cards**?

B Replace the underlined words with your own words and practice again. Be original and creative.

 ## Interactive Practice

A Put the words in appropriate order. Practice aloud with your partner. Do not write.

1. **A:** Did (find / you / OK / everything)?
   B: Yes, thank you. Do you (credit / take / cards / Japanese)?

2. **A:** How long is the (for / this / computer / warranty)?
   B: It's for one year, but you can (it / pay extra / to / extend).

3. **A:** Would you (like / try it / to / on)?
   B: Yes. Where (fitting / is / room / the)?

4. **A:** Can I (you / something / find / help)?
   B: Yes, I'm (for / some / looking / chocolate).

Quick Search on the Web

"Black Friday" and "Cyber Monday" are two days when many shops hold big sales in the U.S. Find out the origins of these names.

Black Friday:
Cyber Monday:

B You're checking out at a cashier at a supermarket. Complete the dialogue with the phrases in the box. Practice with your partner.

> *Thank you. You, too. / Paper or plastic? / Yes, thank you. / Yeah. It's my favorite.*
> *Do you take credit cards? / Pretty good. Thank you. / No, just insert it there.*

Cashier: How're you guys doing?
You: _____

Cashier: Did you find everything all right?
You: _____

Cashier: I like this one too. This is very delicious.
You: _____

Cashier: Your total comes to 11 dollars and 70 cents.
You: _____

Cashier: Sure, we do.
You: OK, here you go.

Cashier: _____
You: Oh, OK.

Cashier: Press OK, the green button, please.
You: Sure.

Cashier: _____
You: A paper bag, please.

Cashier: You guys have a good evening.
You: _____

C You're a salesclerk or a customer at a shop in Japan below. Role-play a dialogue at the following shops. The customer wants to negotiate the price. Start with "May I help you?" Some useful expressions are listed below.

Sales clerk	**Customer**
May I help you?	I'm looking for...?
What are you looking for?	Can I try this on?
That looks nice on you.	How much is this?
That's a good buy.	Can you give me a discount?
Sorry, that's the best price I can give you.	Sorry. I'll think about it and come back.
I'll give it to you for ...yen then.	Do you take credit cards?

At a clothing shop

At a souvenir shop

How to say "No" politely.

Use the phrases "I don't know," or "Let me think about it" when it is difficult to say "No." People will understand that you mean "No." Use one of these phrases to turn down the offer. Practice with your partner.

> *Um, I don't know.*   *Let me think about it.*   *I'll come back later.*

Respond to the conversations below. Practice with your partner.

1. I'll give you a big discount. How about 20 dollars for five?
2. Red is your color. You look really pretty.
3. How do you like these new Nikes?

Active Listening
DL 65   CD2-24

Where are they shopping? Find an appropriate place from the list below.

Store 1 (   ) Store 2 (   ) Store 3 (   ) Store 4 (   )

a. *Grocery store*

b. *Shoe store*

c. *Dollar store*

d. *Open air gift shop*

Active Reading

DL 66   CD2-25

Pair up and take turns reading aloud the following tips for shopping in the U.S. Ask at least two questions to each other.

Here are some important things you may want to keep in mind when you go shopping in the U.S. First, you must have a credit card. You can use a credit card even for buying little things like a can of Coke.

Another thing you may want to keep in mind is that you should be prepared to
5 have a short, friendly chat with cashiers. They may say, "How're you doing?" or "That's a nice choice." Be polite and respond to them. Most Americans enjoy a small casual conversation. You should try to enjoy it, too.

Try to visit a gigantic supermarket. Some supermarkets are so huge that you may feel like you're in an amusement park. You could easily spend a half day
10 there. Small garage sales in the U.S. are also fun. You may find some really unique, old things you'd never find in Japan.

"No frills stores" are also interesting to visit. They are not fancy and have a limited range of goods in cardboard boxes. They may ask you to pay to use the shopping cart (about 25 cents) or you may have to bring your own shopping bags.
15 However, things there tend to be fresh, inexpensive, and eco-friendly.

A Summarize the passage with your partner by filling in the blanks.

If you shop in the U.S., you must have a ¹(   ) because some shops don't take big bills. You should enjoy a casual ²(   ) with cashiers. Be polite and ³(   ) to them. Some supermarkets are so huge that you may feel like you're in an ⁴(   ) park. Small ⁵(   ) sales are also fun. You may find some really unique, old things you would never find in Japan. "No frills stores" are also interesting to visit. They are not ⁶(   ), but things there tend to be fresh and inexpensive.

Quick Search on the Web

Find out more about "garage sales" in the US. Try to find answers to the questions below and share the answers in a small group or with the class.

1. What are other names for garage sales?
2. What kind of items are typically sold at garage sales?
3. How are they advertised?

Activator
Open-ended Practice

A Take turns asking the following questions with your partner. Make sure to add a few comments to your partner's answers.

1. Do you have something you'd like to buy overseas now?

2. Which do you prefer, shopping alone or shopping with your friends?

3. Have you ever negotiated a lower price on something? Were you successful? What was it?

4. Do you often shop online? Which online shops do you often use? Why?

5. What do you think of people who always buy big name brand goods?

6. If your parents gave you 100,000 yen to spend for a suit/dress, which would you like to get, an expensive nice suit/dress or many inexpensive not-so-nice suits/dresses? Why?

7. Tell each other the best or worst shopping experience you have had in your life.

B The biggest purchase in your life could be a house. In a group of three or four, discuss the questions below.

1. At what age do you want to buy your first house? Why?

2. Which would you like to get, a house in the suburbs or a condominium in the city center?

3. How are you going to buy it, by taking out a loan, paying cash, or both?

4. Would you like to get a large inexpensive used house a bit far away from the nearest train station or a small expensive new house near a station?

5. If you become very rich in the future, would you like to get a second house in the mountains or near the beach in Japan or would you rather travel around the world and stay in luxury hotels?

Unit 14 Social Media

Focus

Phone Calls /
Texting

Brainstorm

A Pair up and talk about yourself and your partner. Examples are shown in [ ].

1. **A:** What is your favorite social media app? Why?

   B: I like _____ because _____.

   [Twitter / LINE / Instagram]   [it's easy to use / it has many functions]

2. **A:** How often do you check your text messages?

   B: I check them _____.   [all the time / very often / a few times a day]

3. **A:** How much is your average monthly phone bill?

   B: It's _____ yen.   [less than 2,000 / about 5,000 / more than 8,000]

4. **A:** Which do you like better, talking or texting? Why?

   B: I like _____ better because it's _____.

   [talking / texting]   [easier / quicker / less stressful]

B Switch roles. This time add one or two extra comments. See the example below. Go over 1-4 above. Below is an example for exercise number one.

   A: What is your favorite social media app? Why?

   B: I like LINE the most because it's easy to use.

   A: I agree. How about Instagram? You can see a lot of nice pictures.

   B: I don't like it. It seems like people are bragging about their lives.

Dialogue

Elijah, an international student in Japan, is talking to Hibiki on the phone. Role-play the dialogue with your partner. Then switch roles and practice again.

Elijah: Hello. Is this <u>Erina</u>?

Hibiki: No, this is <u>Hibiki</u>. Her room-mate. She left her cellphone <u>on her bed</u> and went out.

Elijah: Ah... So, you're answering her phone.

Hibiki: Yep. Can I take a message?

Elijah: Yes. Can you tell her that I need her help?

Hibiki: OK, but can I ask what with?

Elijah: Well, I'm thinking about buying <u>a cellphone</u> here in Japan.

Hibiki: Yeah?

Elijah: So, I want her to come along with me to <u>the cellphone shop</u>.

Hibiki: OK. Got it. That's a good idea. I'll let her know.

Elijah: Thank you.

A Ask at least two questions about the dialogue to your partner. Take turns.

B Replace the underlined parts with your own information and practice the conversation again. Change "she" and "her" accordingly. Be original and creative. Try to add a few more lines at the end.

C Listen to the rest of the conversation. Circle either True or False.

1. Elijah's Japanese is very good.   True / False
2. Hibiki was on a study abroad program last year in the U.S.   True / False
3. The assistant that Hibiki talked to on the phone was very helpful.

   True / False
4. Hibiki talked to her Japanese friends in English while she was
   in the U.S.   True / False
5. Elijah seems to be on campus.   True / False

Expressions

🎧 DL 69   💿 CD2-28

A Practice each dialogue with your partner.

1. *A:* **May I speak to** <u>Megumi</u>?
   B: **Speaking/This is** <u>Megumi</u>.

2. *A:* **Call me or text me later.**
   B: I'll DM you on <u>Twitter</u>.

3. *A:* Can we **talk on** <u>Zoom</u>?
   B: No, I'll call you on <u>LINE</u> later.

4. *A:* Thank you for calling ABC Company. **May I help you?**
   B: Yes, **could you put me through to** <u>Ms. Yamamoto</u>, extension <u>5441</u>?

5. *A:* There is no <u>Wahab</u> living here.
   B: Sorry, **I must have the wrong number**.

B Replace the underlined words with your own words and practice again. Be original and creative.

Interactive Practice

A Find the mistakes or inappropriate expressions and replace them with correct or appropriate expressions.

1. *A:* Isn't this 099-1234-5678?
   B: No, you must have the mistake phone.

2. *A:* May I speak to Taku?
   B: I am Taku. Who are you?

3. *A:* Can you tell Reiko can she send me a message in LINE?
   B: Sure.

4. *A:* Do you text, sir?
   B: How old do you think am I? Of course, I do.

Quick Search on the Web

People tend to use informal, shortened language online. What do each of these originally mean? Search each on the web with a partner.

BTW:	FYI:	IMO:
24/7:	FAQ:	W/O:
TBH:	JK:	TL;DR:

B Fill in the blank in A, find the most appropriate response from B, and draw a line. Practice with a partner.

A:

1. Hello, may I _____ to Tanaka-san?   ·
2. You must have the _____ number.   ·
3. This meal would look great on _____. ·
4. Let's chat _____ LINE?   ·
5. What's the most commonly used
   messaging _____ in the U.S.?   ·
6. We spend so much time _____ social
   media.   ·

B:

· Yeah, very Instagrammable.
· I think it's WhatsApp.
· OK. Here is my QR code.
· Sorry. What number is this?
· I know. We're addicted.
· Speaking.

C You were asked to join your friend to do something together this weekend, but you don't want to go. Actually, you don't even like that person. Leave a message with <u>the most unusual reason</u> you can think of on the phone. Pair up and follow the example.

Example

Snowboarding trip to Nagano

A: Hello, Jack? This is Haruka.

B: This is Jack Humbles. Sorry, I'm not available right now. Please leave a message after the beep.

A: Oh, OK. Jack. About the snowboarding trip to Nagano this weekend. Sorry, I can't go. There are two tigers walking around in my neighborhood. It's too dangerous to go out. I'll send you a LINE message later. Sorry.

Shopping in Shibuya

A: Hello, _____. This is _____.

B: This is _____. Sorry, I'm not available right now. Please leave a message after the beep. (beep sound)

A: This is _____. About _____.
I'll send you a LINE message later. Sorry.

Having dinner

A: Hello, _____. This is_____.

B: This is _____. Sorry, I'm not available right now. Please leave a message after the beep. (beep sound)

A: This is _____. About _____.
I'll send you a LINE message later. Sorry.

Communication | Strategy

Rhythm and Intonation > Pronunciation

Rhythm and intonation make a bigger difference than the sounds of each specific word in communication. Do not worry too much about how good your pronunciation is but do pay attention to whether or not your English has good rhythm and intonation.

Try to read the next sentences fast and see if your partner or teacher can understand you?

1. *A:* What's the purpose of your trip? How long are you staying in the U.S.?
   B: 「斎藤寝具店です」(Sight..., ...)
2. *A:* Whose tie is this?
   B: 「いつも会いたい」(It's...)
3. Could you「わしゃ、変」(wash...)? We're having dinner soon.
4. 「ジュマイン・デファイ」(Do...) ask some other friends to come along?
5. Come over here and「知らんぷりー」. (Sit...)

Active Listening

 DL 70   CD2-29

Who is Sakurako talking to? Write down the profession of the person she is talking to.

Conversation 1 _____

Conversation 2 _____

Conversation 3 _____

Conversation 4 _____

Active Reading

DL 71   CD2-30

Pair up and take turns reading the passage about Steve Jobs aloud. Take turns asking at least one question about each paragraph to each other.

The smartphone, something we can't live without, wouldn't exist without Steve Jobs, the founder of the Apple Computer Company. Below is his story and a message you may find inspiring.

5   He dropped out of college after six months because he didn't see the value in it. However, he stayed at the college and audited only the courses that interested him. He slept on the floor of his friend's room and collected empty
10 Coke bottles to get five cents. He was poor. Then, at age 20, he started Apple Computer in the garage at his house. Apple grew into a huge computer company with 4,000 employees within ten years. He was only 30 years old.

However, he was soon kicked out of the company he had built himself. It was painful, but it was good for him to be creative again. He kept doing what he loved.
15 He started companies called NeXT and Pixar, one of the most successful animation companies in the world. He also met his wife, Laurene, during this time.

Then Apple Computer bought NeXT and Steve Jobs returned to Apple, which hadn't put out any new innovative devices since he left. Soon Steve Jobs created the iPod, the iPhone, and the iPad, all of which were huge contributions to technol-
20 ogy globally.

He gave a speech at a university before he died, and he ended his speech with these messages: "Your time is limited, so don't waste it living someone else's life. Have the courage to follow your heart. Keep looking until you find what you love. Don't settle. Stay hungry. Stay foolish."

 A   What do you think about Steve Jobs? Ask these questions to each other.

1. Do you agree that many people are wasting time living someone else's life? If so, give examples.
2. What do you think about his message: "Stay hungry. Stay foolish?"

Quick Search on the Web 🔍

If time allows watch his 15-minute speech at a graduation ceremony at Stanford University together on YouTube. If not, find out more about Laurene, Steve's wife, on the web. She is also a great figure in the world.

Activator
Open-ended Practice

A Interview a partner and find out about your partner's attitudes towards phones or social media. Take notes.

1. What is your favorite social media service? Why?
2. How long was your longest telephone conversation?
3. What did you talk about?
4. What do you think of people using mobile phones on trains?
5. How many hours a day do you think you use your phone on average?
6. How often do you post something on social media?
7. Do you often use stickers in your text messages? Why or why not?
8. If you left your phone at home, and you'd be late for school if you went back. What would you do?
9. Would you answer a phone call from someone you don't know? Why or why not?
10. If your partner (boyfriend/girlfriend) tried to look at your messages on your phone, what would you say?
11. Do you think you could give up social media for a month? A year?

B Make a group of three or four. Take out your mobile phone and choose one picture you want to talk about. Show the picture to the members of your group. Talk for about 30 seconds about the picture. Try to answer any questions your group members may have about the picture.

Focus

Exchanging Ideas and Opinions

Brainstorm

A Pair up and talk about yourself and your partner. Examples are shown in [   ].

1. *A:* Do you know what SDGs stands for?
   B: I think it stands for _____.   [Sustainable Development Goals]

2. *A:* How many goals and targets are there in SDGs?
   B: I think there are _____ goals and _____
   targets.   [17 / 169]

3. *A:* Can you name some of the goals?
   B: Let's see. They are _____.
   [Zero hunger / Gender equality / Climate action, ...]

4. *A:* Are you doing anything to help achieve these goals?
   B: Yes, I always try to _____.
   [buy eco-friendly food / pick up garbage on street]

B Switch roles. This time add one or two extra comments. See the example below. Go over 1-4 above again. Below is an example for exercise number one.

   A: Do you know what SDGs stands for?
   B: I think it stands for Sustainable Development Goals.
   A: <u>What do you think of these goals?</u>
   B: <u>They are important, but I don't think we can achieve all of them goals by 2030.</u>
   A: <u>You may be right, but we need them to create a better, fairer world.</u>
   B: <u>No doubt about it!</u>

 # Dialogue

🎧 DL 72   💿 CD2-31

Gerry and Kenji just came out of a class on SDGs. They are talking more after class. Role-play the dialogue with your partner. Then switch roles and practice again.

Gerry: What do you think of the Global Goals?

Ai: You means SDGs?

Gerry: Yes.

Ai: Well, I think they're important, but I don't know what I can do myself.

Gerry: That's what a lot of people say.

Ai: Well, at least I could try to <u>turn off the lights when leaving a room</u>.

Gerry: Good. That helps <u>save energy</u>.

Ai: It does, doesn't it? How about you?

Gerry: Let's see. I could <u>learn more about issues affecting women</u>.

Ai: Are you talking about <u>gender equality</u>?

Gerry: Of course.

A Ask at least two questions about the dialogue to your partner. Take turns.

B Replace the underlined parts with your own information and practice the conversation again. Be original and creative. Try to add a few more lines at the end.

C Listen to the rest of the conversation. Complete the summary by filling in the blanks with appropriate words listed below.   🎧 DL 73   💿 CD2-32

> *tsuma   better half   independent   homemaker*
> *yome   housewife   negative*

Gerry is a big supporter of gender equality. He knows that March 8th is International Women's Day. He also tries not to use the words like "[1](   )" in English or "okusan" in Japanese. He thinks "[2](   )" is a better word than housewife. "Homemaker" sounds more [3](   ). Gerry thinks married women should be equal to their partners. Kenji suggested the use of "[4](   )" instead of "okusan," but Gerry thinks that that is even worse. Then he suggested the use of "[5](   )." In English, they sometimes use words such as "partner" or "[6](   )" or even "honey." Gerry believes we shouldn't use any words that sound [7](   ) towards women. Kenji agreed.

 # Expressions

A Practice each dialogue with your partner.

1. **A: Why don't we** stop using <u>electricity</u> at home?
   B: I think that's <u>a bad</u> idea.

2. **A: Tell me your opinions on** <u>giving money to homeless people</u>?
   B: Well, <u>it depends</u>. I think it can be good and bad.

3. **A: I don't think** we can <u>achieve all the SDGs</u>.
   B: You never know. At least everybody should try hard.

4. **A: What did you think about** <u>the speech</u>?
   B: It was OK. I wasn't really <u>impressed</u>.

5. **A:** We should bring home our own trash.
   B: I have to disagree. We <u>need more garbage cans on the street</u>.

B Replace the underlined words with your own words and practice again. Be original and creative.

 # Interactive Practice

A Let's review what the Global Goals are. Here are the first 11 of 17 goals. Pair up and make sure you know what they all mean. Discuss with a partner or as a class.

1. No Poverty
2. Zero Hunger
3. Good Health and Wellbeing
4. Quality Education
5. Gender Equality
6. Clean Water and Sanitation
7. Affordable and Clean Energy
8. Decent Work and Economic Growth
9. Industry, Innovation, and Infrastructure
10. Reduced Inequalities
11. Sustainable Cities and Communities

Quick Search on the Web

There are several specific "targets" to achieve each goal. Choose one goal from the above and list at least two specific targets for that goal. Report what you find to your partner.

1:

2:

B Below are some words or phrases for giving comments and/or opinions. Group them into three categories: Positive, Neutral, and Negative.

> *Fascinating / terrible / exciting / so-so / not too bad /*
> *boring / wonderful / awesome / silly / fair /*
> *I don't know / I love it / I don't like it / I completely agree with you /*
> *I have to disagree / I have no idea*

Positive	Neutral	Negative

C Give comments or opinions on the statements using one of the words or phrases you learned in exercise **B**. Number one is done for you.

1. *A:* What do you think of donating our unwanted clothes to an NPO.
   B: <u>Hey, that's an excellent idea</u>. <u>It makes us happy, and they'll be happy, too.</u>

2. *A:* How would you like going to India to do some volunteer work this winter with me?
   B: Well, to be honest, I _____. _____.

3. *A:* We should try not to use detergent when we wash dishes.
   B: I think that's _____ idea. _____.

4. *A:* I don't like people who judge others by their appearance.
   B: I _____. _____.

5. *A:* We should increase the budget for military spending to keep peace.
   B: I _____. _____.

6. *A:* What do you think about <u>(your own idea)</u> _____?
   B: I _____. _____.

Communication Strategy

Say "I" first

Say "I" immediately after questions without thinking what you want to say and then add others necessary. Surprisingly this magic "I" will help you pull out the expressions or phrases you need. Practice with your partner.

1. **A:** What would you do if you had one million yen?
   B: I, I, I, I would _____.
2. **A:** What do you think of students who sleep in class?
   B: I, I, I, I think they _____.
3. **A:** Is it really that bad to eat whale meat?
   B: I, I, I, I think _____.

Active Listening

 DL 75   CD2-34

Almost thirty years ago, at the Earth Summit in Rio de Janeiro, Brazil, Severn Suzuki, a 12-year-old from Canada made a speech. It's only a six-minute speech, but it was so powerful that it awakened the whole world to doing something to make the world fair, peaceful, and environmentally friendly with no hungry children and no war. Listen to a portion of her speech twice and complete the summary below.

You, adults teach children not to fight with others, to ¹(   ) others and to clean up our mess. Then, why do you go out and do the things you tell us not to do? You don't know how to fix the ²(   ) in our ozone layer. You don't know how to bring back an ³(   ) now extinct. If you don't know how to fix it, please stop breaking it! I'm only a child, yet I know we should act as one single world towards one single goal.

One ⁴(   ) I met on a street in Rio yesterday told us: "If I were rich, I would give all the street children ⁵(   ), clothes, medicine, shelter and love." If a child on the street who has nothing, is willing to share, why are we who have everything still so ⁶(   )? I'm only a child, yet I know if all the money spent on ⁷(   ) was spent on ending poverty and finding environmental answers, what a wonderful place this earth would be!

Active Reading

🎧 DL 76   ◎ CD2-35

Pair up and read the passage about the UN'S Global Goals called SDGs.

The Sustainable Development Goals are a map to achieve a better and more sustainable future for all. They address global challenges such as poverty, in-
5 equality, climate change, environmental degradation, peace, and justice. It is important that we leave no one behind and that we achieve them all by 2030. Some of the goals are as follows.

10 **1.** No Poverty: Access to (   ) human needs of health, education, sanitation
2. Zero Hunger: Providing (   ) and humanitarian relief, establishing sustainable food production
3. Good Health and Wellbeing: Better and more accessible health systems to increase (   )
15 **4.** Quality Education: Inclusive education to enable upward (   ) mobility and end poverty
5. Gender Equality: Education regardless of gender, advancement of equality laws, fairer representation of (   )
6. Clean Water and (   ): Improving access for billions of people
20 who lack these basic facilities

A Work together with a partner to fill in the blanks with appropriate words listed below.

life-expectancy   women   social   sanitation   basic   food

Quick Search on the Web 🔍

Find out what some well-known companies such as Starbucks, MacDonald's, Toyota, etc. are doing to help achieve some of the 17 goals. Report your findings in a small group in English.

Example

I found out that Toyota has been trying to realize the SDG philosophy of "No one will be left behind" by providing "Mobility for All: freedom of movement for all." Thanks to this, seniors and disabled people may have a better chance of moving around outside.

Activator
Open-ended Practice

A Stand up and move around. Find out to what degree your classmates agree with the statements below. If you have someone who <u>strongly agrees</u> with the statements write down that classmate's name.

A: We should not waste food. What do you think?

B: I totally agree with you. In fact, I always eat all the food on the table.

A: Good. May I have your name?

B: Mari.　　　　　　　　　　　　　　　　　(　　　　Mari　　　　)

We should...　　　　　　　　　　　　　　**List of Names**

- use eco-friendly bags. What do you think?　　(　　　　　　　　)
- bike, walk, or take public transportation to school.　(　　　　　　　　)
- do some volunteer work at least once a week.　(　　　　　　　　)
- reduce, reuse, and recycle as much as possible.　(　　　　　　　　)
- donate money or support the "$2-a-day challenge."　(　　　　　　　　)
- post about women's rights or climate changes on social media.

　　　　　　　　　　　　　　　　　　　　(　　　　　　　　)

- shop local. Support neighborhood businesses.　(　　　　　　　　)
- take short showers. Baths require too much water.　(　　　　　　　　)

B Even a lazy person can do something to save the world. Discuss in small groups what else we can do to end poverty, fight inequality and injustice, and fix climate change. Then make a 15-second speech about something you can start to help save the world.

I'm just a regular, lazy college student, and I thought I cannot do much, but I think even I can still do something small. I've decided to start a 30-day-challenge. My challenge is to "Not eat too much." You may laugh, but this will help save food, and I can lose weight too. Thank you.

| 本書には音声 CD（別売）があります |

Activator Next

大学生の自信を促す英語コミュニケーション

2023年1月20日　初版第1刷発行
2023年3月31日　初版第3刷発行

著　者　　塩　澤　　正
　　　　　Adam Martinelli

発行者　　福　岡　正　人
発行所　　株式会社　金　星　堂
（〒101-0051）東京都千代田区神田神保町 3-21
Tel. (03) 3263-3828（営業部）
(03) 3263-3997（編集部）
Fax (03) 3263-0716
https://www.kinsei-do.co.jp

編集担当　稲葉真美香　　　　　　　　　Printed in Japan
印刷所・製本所／三美印刷株式会社
本書の無断複製・複写は著作権法上での例外を除き禁じられ
ています。本書を代行業者等の第三者に依頼してスキャンや
デジタル化することは、たとえ個人や家庭内での利用であっ
ても認められておりません。
落丁・乱丁本はお取り替えいたします。

ISBN978-4-7647-4178-2　C1082